D0283206

liturgies for children

liturgies for children

by Andrew Jamison

Nihil Obstat:
    Rev. Hilarion Kistner, O.F.M.
    Rev. John Jennings

Imprimi Potest:
    Rev. Godfrey Blank, O.F.M.
    Vicar Provincial

Imprimatur:
    +Joseph L. Bernardin
    Archbishop of Cincinnati
    February 7, 1975

The *Nihil Obstat* and *Imprimatur* are a declaration that a book or pamphlet is considered
to be free from doctrinal or moral error. It is not implied that those who have granted the
Nihil Obstat and *Imprimatur* agree with the contents, opinions or statements expressed.

Cover and illustrations by Kieran Quinn

SBN 0-912228-18-0

CONTENTS

II. SCHOOL SITUATIONS

III. SEASONS OF THE YEAR

Advent

Christmas

Lent

Easter

IV. FIRST COMMUNION—PENANCE

APPENDIX

ACKNOWLEDGMENTS

A child asked an artist, "How long did it take you to paint that picture?" The artist replied, "Five minutes and my whole lifetime." I want to thank those lifetime contributors — relatives and friends who have made me the person I am — special people like Mom and Dad, "D.J.," Bob and Carol, Dale, Alan and Sue, Jim, Donna, Tod, Marie, Pat and Tom, and Bernard.

The five minutes of my life are really the five years I've enjoyed with the people of Emporia as their friend and priest. This book grew with the children of Sacred Heart Parish: Anne, Veronica, Chris, Ricky, Jeff, Victor, Mike, Patsy, Mary Aileene, David, Leslie, Kevin, Cassie.

The two people to whom I am indebted for the initial idea to write this book are Gail Milton and Nancy Hoffmans. Their encouragement, work and suggestions were invaluable.

The culmination of many lived experiences, this book needed the support of Father Lambert Dannenfelser, O.F.M., former pastor; Father Raymar Middendorf, O.F.M., present pastor; the Precious Blood Sisters of Wichita, Kansas, who teach in our School of Religion; Sister Marie Zoglman, A.S.C., Sister Dionysia Stump, A.S.C., Jeanne Antram, Patricia Walterscheid and Mary Kay Kriley who are responsible for developing many of these liturgies.

I want to thank those who were instrumental in the book's taking final form: Jeanne Heiman, Beverly Toso, Mary Kay Kriley, Maxine Gasso, Marcia Rues, John Sterbenz, Susan Murphy, Father Harold Schneider, Gloria Saar, Margaret Hughes and Jo Ellen Greischaar. I am also grateful to Barbara Beckwith, assistant editor of St. Anthony Messenger, who did the final editing, assisted by Robert Buescher, O.F.M.

Introduction

This book is about children's liturgies: what they are, how to prepare for them, and how to execute them. The liturgies are intended for grades one through six. The same liturgical process can be used with children of other ages as well.

Let's begin by admitting that our Christian religion is an adult religion. To my way of thinking, only adults are able to make a complete act of faith in God, to really believe in him in the sense that they comprehend better the meaning of a lifelong commitment. Adults receive the motivation and support for their faith through the liturgy. You ask: Where does that leave the child?

Often our liturgies on Sunday or during the week are geared specifically to adults. Not only are many of the words and symbols of the Mass beyond children, but the Word Preached is also on an adult level. I, for one, aim my Sunday homilies at adult ears, and hope to catch the children through examples that may relate to them.

Christianity is transmitted to children through adults. They come into contact with religion not just at Sunday Mass but in the whole life-style *(weltanschauung)* of their parents. As Catholic columnist Dolores Curran puts it:

There's a movement on to disregard God until the child can understand him, at 12 or so. This is wrong. We need to disregard doctrine until a child can abstract it, but not God. Children need to believe in a Supreme Being, in a loving God, and in parents who represent that God to them. One of the best catechism lessons we can give children is a loving set of parents who allow the light of Christ to shine in their lives.

Even though children cannot understand what a commitment to faith really entails, we can at least introduce them to the community of adult believers. Just as children might become interested in baseball or music or books because of their parent's example, so also youngsters learn to appreciate their religion through the commitment of their parents.

Parents are the basic models for the way a child feels about God. For this reason the *Directory for Masses with Children* challenges parents and teachers to coordinate their efforts:

All who have a part in the formation of children should consult and work together. In this way even if children already have some feeling about God and the things of God, they may also experience the human values which are found in the eucharistic celebration, depending upon their age and personal progress. These values are the activity of the community, exchange of greetings, capacity to listen and to seek and grant pardon, expression of gratitude, experience of symbolic actions, a meal of friendship, and festive celebration. (No. 9, Directory for Masses with Children, *Sacred Congregation for Divine Worship, United States Catholic Conference, Washington, D.C., November 1, 1973)*

When we begin to zero in specifically on the Mass, we have to be careful that we give children what they are able to handle. Very often, the Sunday Mass means nothing to them because they cannot see the priest's actions, they cannot understand the words, or they are more interested in what they are going to eat later for breakfast than in homilies on charity, school finances or the place of the eschatological Christ in our lives.

Dolores Curran refers to this situation:

We need to face up to the fact that either children should not attend [Sunday Mass], or that if they do, we give them something to which they can relate.

The Mass should try to fit the age and mentality of the children. Through the principal rites and prayers, it should convey its meaning including a participation in the whole life of the Church, according to the *Directory* (No. 12).

Attractive Liturgies Nourish Faith

The U.S. Bishops' Committee on the Liturgy spelled out our need to celebrate and a theology of celebration: liturgies are intended "to give bodily expression to faith, to transform our fragile awareness of Christ's presence in the dark of our daily isolation into a joyful, integral experience of his liberating action in the solidarity of the celebrating community." It is clear, therefore, that the manner in which the Church celebrates the liturgy affects our faith. As the committee concludes, "Good celebrations foster and nourish faith. Poor celebrations weaken and destroy faith."

Liturgies on every level are to be attractive, human experiences. The God we worship has become one of us; he chose to reveal himself in our history and our lives. Our liturgies then should deal with our experiences, and deal with them in a humanly pleasing way. The attractiveness comes about when the liturgy is able to relate to us, when it finds a vehicle, tool, method or "gimmick" to get across the Christian message. If we can start with a human experience, we have a good chance of discovering the God who stands under our experience.

Attention-getters or "gimmicks" are attractive to children. They have difficulty dealing with abstract concepts like "Kingdom of God," "thanksgiving," John the Baptist "preparing" the way of the Lord. But if someone can make a difficult concept *concrete*

3

through an attention-getter, he is preparing the children for the heart of the Christian message.

Groundwork is necessary to pre-evangelize the children. For example, in talking of our "response" to Jesus during the Christmas season, I used a string of Christmas tree lights with three different kinds of bulbs: *lighted* ones to signify those of us who follow Jesus (our light burns bright); *blinking* ones to indicate a half-hearted response to Jesus; and *burned-out* ones to show those people who have turned Jesus off. The lighted bulbs can be linked with the paschal mystery of life/death by commenting that Jesus is our light and our life and even his dying cannot make the light flicker. In fact, he dies only to rise, and it is this death/resurrection that makes our light bright. In the Mass he gives this light to us so that we too can shine brightly.

Gimmicks, like Christmas bulbs, drama, flowers, balloons and other audio-visuals, focus the attention of the children on the concrete — their level for understanding. The child's perceptions are unique — the child will structure life his or her own way, and teachers help facilitate this experience. We begin with the senses, with objects, and then proceed to mysteries. The use of audio-visuals, drama, dialogues, etc., has the ability to slow life down so that we concentrate on a small section of it. Then we pinpoint the essence of truth and see that this essence partakes of the mystery of the Way, the Christian outlook on life realized through our grasping of the death/resurrection pattern of Christ.

In the preaching guide, *Good News,* Rev. Joseph T. Nolan observes that the secret of preaching is to talk of simple things from everyday experience and to "see" them for the first time, in relation to the pain and joy and deeper rhythms of death and life. Jesus used this secret first. His preaching and parables often develop simple incidents like running short of food and drink, unexpected guests coming, borrowing from the neighbors, losing money, throwing a party, and needing a drink of cool, delicious water on a hot day. (These are all Gospel scenes — do you recognize them?)

This book on children's liturgies is an attempt to tell this secret of the Good News to all people, especially children, in a way they can grasp. Our children's liturgies at Sacred Heart Parish in Emporia, Kansas, involve the children from the parochial

4

elementary school and the elementary CCD program (and sometimes both groups together). In planning these liturgies I have found certain ways of working profitable. I would like to present a few ideas on how themes for children's liturgies emerge, and then discuss the mechanics of applying those themes.

Liturgy Starts in the Here and Now

"Each eucharistic celebration with children should be carefully prepared beforehand . . . in discussion with the adults and with the children who will have a special ministry in these Masses," the *Directory* (No. 29) insists.

To start this process, I try to contact the *present,* the here-and-now experiences of the children. I ask a group of six to 10 children questions like: What happened to you this past weekend? What was your saddest experience last week? What made you happy yesterday? By concentrating on the recent experiences of the children, I can discover what has impressed them lately. What one child says usually plugs into the experiences of another one, and we have the makings of a theme.

This approach is preferable to asking directly, "All right, kids, what's going to be our theme for the Mass Thursday?" "The Spirit," Michael may say. "How about free days?" interrupts Mark. "Let's talk about my dead dog," Connie suggests. "Cocoa puffs," says Donald. "Love," mentions Mary. The point-blank question usually spawns a litany of one or two word answers, often too general to be workable, and not always pertinent to the entire group. Sometimes a good idea emerges; often the group wants to talk about other things.

For this reason it's wise to suggest some structure to help the children center in on a theme.

In addition, the tendency in working on a theme is to get right down to selecting the songs, assigning children for the different roles, and working out the mechanics immediately. A more satisfactory approach to liturgy planning combines what I call "selecting a theme" or "searching for a theme," with the working out of the mechanics.

5

First Method: Selecting a Theme

In "selecting a theme" the theme arises early in the discussion or is imposed upon the group. Often, the time of the liturgy makes a theme self-evident. For instance, a liturgy for the week before Mother's Day would have the natural theme, "Mothers." If the kids are thinking about their Halloween costumes and preparations for trick-or-treat, why not invite them to plan an "All Hallows" liturgy emphasizing all saints? Themes of beginning and ending are pertinent at the opening or closing of the school year.

Where national holidays, religious holydays and special events in the city or nation are common experiences for everyone, the theme may emerge spontaneously. It's easy to center in on a theme when your city just had a power failure, or the river flooded, or the children dislike the school lunch program, for example. The sharing of common experiences is a basis for liturgical sharing.

What becomes more difficult is the problem of "fleshing out" the theme once it's selected. How do you take the theme, "Mothers," and make it relate to the children before you? How do you get them to speak freely of their feelings about their mothers in a way that can be useful for the liturgy?

I had primary children to work with in preparing a liturgy for the Thursday before Mother's Day. First of all, I had them write down their mothers' names on a piece of paper. Then I asked them: What one thing did you enjoy doing with your mom this past weekend? They responded:

washing dishes
cleaning the house
mowing the lawn
crying with her when we were in an accident
miss her, for she was gone this past weekend
going out to eat with her
golfing with her

The two answers I thought most significant were: crying with her and missing her.

Starting with these answers we discussed how we feel when we are around our mothers. Someone mentioned that he sometimes got mad at his mother. Since this kind of anger seemed to be a common experience among the children, we talked about

6

how we often blow our stacks at our mothers, and whether this is good or bad. We compared ourselves to a bottle of coke that we shake up and put our thumbs over the top. When we get all shook up, we want to explode and spill over just like that bottle of coke. Sometimes we do this to our mothers, and we're sorry for it; but our mothers still love us and we're happy about that. We want to show our love for our mothers on this Mother's Day.

This example explains the process that our liturgy planning team (8 second graders, 2 first graders) had to go through *before* we could continue with our planning. This "fleshing out" of the theme is a necessary process to work through with the children; otherwise, they do not have any experience to hook onto when they participate in the liturgy. The theme has not only been selected; it has grown out of the experiences of the children and been enlarged through their eyes and ears and mouths.

Second Method: Searching for a Theme

Sometimes a theme is not obvious. We have to dig for it by delving into the here-and-now experiences of the children. One effective way is to divide the class in two and let each child in one group write about a happy experience he or she had in the last two days, each child in the other group, a sad experience. Depending on what emerges, many themes are now possible, themes ranging from an illness in a family to mommy and daddy's fighting.

To give an example, our school had a "crazy hat day" when the students could wear any kind of hat they wanted. From talking about hats at the beginning of the liturgy planning session (that's where the minds of the students were), we drifted onto the topic of clothes in general. We talked about the fact that sometimes we dress up; sometimes we want to wear old jeans. Clothes help us impress people; they can be a coverup, and tell people we're something we really aren't.

From these comments the children pointed out various ways that they themselves judge people by the clothes they wear or don't wear. After our discussion we decided to celebrate our conclusions: "It's what's on the inside that counts" and "Looks are only skin deep." Those two phrases developed into a poster, and our theme became "It's what's on the inside that counts."

7

In both methods, "selecting a theme" and "searching for a theme," what was important was not so much the fact that we arrived at a theme, but the process we went through. One half to three quarters of our liturgy planning time is devoted to this process of discussing or searching for a theme. In this way, the students become aware of what this liturgy is intended to do and how it applies to their lives.

Bringing It All Together

There are many more things that should be done once you have specified the theme of the Mass. Now is the time to get the children involved in the proximate preparation for the liturgy (Cf. *Directory,* No. 22). I find it worthwhile to involve children in selecting and presenting the readings, composing the apology (penitential rite) and the general intercessions, making visual aids like banners and posters, illustrating the homily by presenting skits, selecting the place for the liturgy and deciding who is to be invited.

These activities can all go on simultaneously by dividing your class or liturgy planning group into smaller interest groups. With the assistance of another adult, one group can select the readings and readers; another can choose the songs; another can compose the introduction to the Mass and general intercessions, etc.

With intermediate students one method of selecting and emphasizing the readings is to present three Scripture passages to a group of five children and ask them to select two readings. (I generally tell primary students which readings we'll use.) They are to read the readings to themselves, then share the most significant passage they discovered in each reading with the rest of the group. Finally the group selects two people as lectors for the Mass. This way gives students the chance to delve into Scripture more and learn to understand what is there.

When the small groups have completed their tasks, we bring the whole class together to share our results. The completed project, from choosing the theme to the last letter on a poster, may involve three or four get-togethers with the children. Undeniably the process takes time, but in my experience the effects are long-lasting too. Now we are ready for the celebration itself. Both children and adults have practiced, know what they are to do, and can enjoy the Eucharist.

What Can Teachers And Celebrants Do?

For school liturgies the teachers quite often are able to pinpoint relevant Mass themes for their classes. They can help lead various groups in preparing: for instance, a teacher could work with the group in composing the prayers of the faithful or the penitential rite. For Sunday liturgies, interested adults and teachers can help practice timing, cues and speaking with the children on the Saturday before.

The celebrant can also help practice, but basically he is the liturgy facilitator or coordinator, in addition to planning the homily and the general instructions that provide the transition from experience to worship. "It is the responsibility of the priest who celebrates with children to make the celebration festive, fraternal, meditative" (*Directory,*No. 23). Much of the success of a celebration depends on how comfortable the celebrant feels around children, what preparation he has made, and how he acts and speaks. Children sense the willingness to communicate that a celebrant shows.

Children find introductory remarks before various parts of the liturgy especially helpful. The celebrant may want to expand on the theme of apology during the penitential rite, for example, or introduce the preface and emphasize the words that relate to the Mass theme.

The homily should be given great prominence in all Masses with children (Cf. *Directory*, No. 48). A dialogue between the priest and children often brings out the practical aspects of the theme. If the celebrant finds it difficult to adapt himself to the mentality of children, however, another adult may speak to them, with the consent of the pastor (Cf. *Directory,* No. 24). A sister, teacher, deacon, brother—any of these could assume this role.

Our liturgy preparation sessions are actually religion classes for the individual class chosen to prepare the liturgy for their level. Preparation creates interest and helps the youngsters realize that the liturgy can relate to their everyday lives. By enabling them to participate in the planning and execution of the liturgy, they are

9

preparing for their future roles as parish liturgical leaders. If they become comfortable in public worship and develop an eagerness to work on a liturgy and participate, these children have acquired a religious experience that was not available to us when we were their age.

Through our children or the young men and women with whom we work, we too will be renewed in our own faith. We will be a "recycled" Christian who will again be alive and living in the Church.

How to Use This Book

I view this book as a *resource* and a *creative educational* tool. As a *resource* book, it consists of planned liturgies that have *worked* with elementary school children and adults who also participate. (Interestingly, adults sometimes gain as much from these liturgies as their children. Some parents hold themselves aloof, but they begin to respond to the liturgy as they see their children participating and enjoying it.) This book is essentially a *resource* for homily hints, attractive music and the development of a theme. Any of these liturgies may be used as written.

As a *creative educational* book, it provides the tools to prepare and compose your own liturgies. The finished liturgies come easily when you've gone through the process of developing a theme and planning the variables.

Children are a resource for the liturgy. They are seldom different from adults—they are sad and happy, successful and failing, selfish and generous. Children's liturgies try to speak in simpler and more concrete language than what parents can grasp. The child has a certain uncontaminated sense of wonder and ability to praise God wholeheartedly. This spirit surfaces in children's liturgies and calls out the best in us adults. Perhaps we can wonder and praise with them.

Here are a set of "Beatitudes" that highlight both the tension and joy of working with children's liturgies:
1. Blessed are those who are patient with problems and obstacles to liturgy planning; God shall be ever patient with them.
2. Blessed are those who move *gradually*—adequately and in

10

ample time *preparing* people for changes; they are less apt to "blow the whole thing."

3. Blessed are they who, on the other hand, are not afraid to jump into deep water (be willing to take a few risks); a Life Preserver shall be awaiting them.

4. Blessed are they who guide their children to do their own liturgy planning; some day they shall be able to "just sit back" (and with happy results).

5. Blessed are they who keep in mind the liturgical season, in which is contained the thread binding days together; their liturgies shall not fall apart.

6. Blessed are they who remember that children are VERBS, not NOUNS; they shall provide enough gestures, postures and activities that their little worshippers will grow closer to their Source of Life.

7. Blessed are they who think *concretely* rather than *abstractly*; the visual aids, posters and symbols they provide will produce vivid imagery, reaping lasting fruit.

8. Blessed are they who become like little children; of such is the Kingdom of God.

May this book be your "diving board" into exploring the rich waters of God's presence in the lives of his children.

I General Themes

1. FLYING HIGH WITH GOD

Background: The children on the intermediate level wanted to compose a liturgy that would emphasize getting high on God rather than on drugs or alcohol. To highlight this theme, children brought to Mass paper kites they made. The kites were not flown but used as posters.

Opening Hymn: "Blowing in the Wind"

Reading I: Romans 8: 11-18 (The Spirit replaces sin in us by emphasizing "everyone moved by the Spirit is a Son of God.")

Reading II: An excerpt from Richard Bach's *Jonathan Livingston Seagull,* Avon Books, 1970, pp. 39-40. (Jonathan follows a higher purpose in life.)

Reading III: Matthew 6: 25-34 (Since God takes care of the birds of the air, how much more us!)

Homily Hints: The seagull, Jonathan Livingston, is similar to a kite, for gliding above the earth brings a certain independence. Dependence on drugs, alcohol, needles and airplane glue takes away our freedom.
    In this Mass, Jesus gives us real strength and power to fly high with God.

Offertory Hymn: "You Fill the Day"

Recessional: "Spirit of God"

2. HAPPINESS IS . . .

Background: Snoopy and Peanuts are familiar characters to children and create automatic interest. So, for this liturgy, we used the "happiness is" theme.

Opening Hymn: "Joy, Joy, Joy"

Penitential Rite:
    Lector: For the times we have teased or made someone sad,
    All: We are sorry, Lord.
    Lector: For the times we did not share our toys with others,
    All: We are sorry, Lord.
    Lector: For the times we were angry at our parents,
    All: We are sorry, Lord.
    Lector: For the times we did not thank someone who gave us something good,
    All: We are sorry, Lord.
    Lector: For the times we could have made someone happy — and didn't,
    All: We are sorry, Lord.

Reading I: Psalm 104: 10-15 (The providence of God to nature and man, "wine to make them cheerful, oil to make their faces shine and bread to make their hearts strong."

Responsorial Psalm: Psalm 100: 1-5 (adapted for children)
    Lector: Shout with joy before the Lord, O earth!
    All: Shout with joy before the Lord, O earth!
    Lector: Obey him gladly, come before him, singing with joy.
    All: Shout with joy before the Lord, O earth!
    Lector: Try to understand what this means — the Lord is God!
        He made us — we are his people, the sheep of his
        pasture.
    All: Shout with joy before the Lord, O earth!
    Lector: Go through his open doors with many thanks. Go into
        his church with praise. Give thanks to him and bless
        his name.
    All: Shout with joy before the Lord, O earth!
    Lector: For the Lord is always good. He is always loving and
        kind. He has been good to our fathers and
        grandfathers as well as to us.
    All: Shout with joy before the Lord, O earth!

Reading II: Luke 12: 22-24,27-31 (Don't worry, God will provide for
us like the birds of the air and the flowers.)

Reading III: Matthew 5: 1-10 (The Sermon on the Mount, "How
happy the poor in spirit; theirs is the Kingdom of
heaven.")

Homily Hints: I used the familiar magazine section from the
Sunday newspaper and turned the pages to find
"happiness" there. This is what I discovered: a
Peanuts cartoon by Charles Schultz about Lucy
selling happiness for "five cents, please"; a large
box of cereal (Cocoa Puffs, Cheerios). I want
something, and I want it now. Can we buy
happiness?

    Happiness is sharing — by letting others play in
our games, by watching mom as she buys you a pair
of shoes, even though she could use a pair herself.

    Happiness is like swimming in water because it is
all around us and embraces us even in the middle of
trials and sad times.

    Happiness is when the Father shared Jesus with
us and shares him again today.

Prayers of the Faithful:

Happiness is bubblegum and pop.
Response: Thank you, Lord.
Happiness is Sesame Street and a big teddy bear. (Response)
Happiness is going to the circus and having popcorn.
(Response)
Happiness is a new basketball goal. (Response)
Happiness is going to a party in a new dress. (Response)
Happiness is daddy coming home from work. (Response)
Happiness is knowing God loves me. (Response)

Offertory Hymn: "Kum Ba Ya"

Communion Hymn: "They'll Know We Are Christians"

Recessional: "Joy, Joy, Joy"

3. GROWTH IN LIVING

Background: This liturgy highlights the different stages of development we can be in. It emphasizes the continual giving of oneself to the Lord and can be tied in with the physical growth of children.

Opening Hymn: "Here We Are" (Our present stance before the Lord)

Penitential Rite Response: Lord have mercy. Help us to grow!

Reading I: Romans 13:11-13 (We must change our evil ways, "Cast off the works of darkness and put on the armor of light.")

Reading II: Mark 4:1-20 (Parable of the sower and the seed)

Homily Hints: Use an exhibit to illustrate your point. In a previous week, have some children begin growing flower or vegetable seeds in water, soil, absorbent cotton, gravel, etc. This exhibit should illustrate the parable well and the way we should be receptive to God's word and work.

Offertory Hymn: "I Have Decided to Follow Jesus"

Communion Hymn: "Be a New Man"

Recessional: To re-emphasize the continual commitment to the Lord, sing the song "Put Your Hand in the Hand."

4. BEHAVIOR

Background: The intermediate grades composed this liturgy after reflecting on a familiar behavior pattern — how we use other people to get what we want. Children may not use the sophisticated word "manipulation," but they know what it means on the experiential level.

Opening Hymn: "They'll Know We Are Christians"

Reading I: Genesis 3: 1-12 (Adam blames Eve for his sin.)

Reading II: 1 John 3: 15-19 (Love people by your actions, "My children, our love is not to be just words or mere talk, but something real and active.")

Reading III: Mark 10: 13-16 (Jesus loves little children, "Let the children come to me; do not stop them; for it is to such as these that the Kingdom of God belongs.")

Homily Hints: Two creative children composed a skit to illustrate our theme and presented it here. They dramatized a

familiar home situation: a son approaches his mother and asks if he can vacuum the floor, wash the dishes, and empty the trash. Then he asks for $1.50 so he can go to the movies and buy some candy.

From this initial example, the homilist can help the children reflect on other examples of how our actions and behaviors sometime hide our true motives.

Ask the children: What is Jesus trying to say to us by his giving himself to us in communion?

Offertory: silent

Communion Hymn: "Be a New Man"

Recessional: "The Mass Is Ended"

5. MOTHERS (1)

Background: The primary children chose "mother" as a theme after mentioning the idea many times. They invited their mothers to attend the liturgy which took place in their classroom.

Opening Hymn: "Praise the Lord"

Reading I: Luke 1: 26-28 (The Annunciation — Mary consents to be the mother of Jesus.)

Reading II: John 19: 26-27 (Jesus gives Mary to St. John as his mother.)

Homily Hints: Produce a large candy bar and share it with the children now. Explain that just as you shared the candy with them, so also mothers share their love.

Jesus shares so much that he not only gave us his mother but also gives us his Body and Blood.

Offertory Hymn: "Simple Gifts"

Communion Hymn: "We All Need One Another"

Recessional: "The Mass Is Ended"

6. MOTHERS (2)

Background: Since mothers are notoriously soft-hearted, children usually seek them out first whenever they want something. This liturgy encourages our respect and appreciation for what our mothers tell us.

Opening Hymn: "Here We Are"

Penitential Rite: Celebrant: One wintry day when I was young I remember my Mom asking me to change my scout uniform before I went out to visit a friend. She said she didn't want me to tear my uniform or get it dirty. "I won't mess it up, Mom," I said. Well, I slipped on the ice and tore my knee. Mom was upset, and I felt bad. Let's stop and think back to apologize for those things we have done wrong.

Lector: We are sorry for not obeying our parents.

All: Lord, forgive us.

Lector: We are sorry for yelling at our brothers and sisters and teasing them, just because we're in a bad mood.

All: Lord, forgive us.

Lector: We are sorry for being lazy at home and not taking care of our household jobs.

All: Lord, forgive us.

Celebrant: Jesus tells us that if we are sorry, he is able to forgive us in the name of the Father, and of the Son, and of the Holy Spirit. Amen.

Reading I: Luke 18: 15-17 (Mothers bring children to Jesus, "People even brought little children to Jesus for him to touch.")

Reading II: Luke 2: 41-52 (The story of Jesus lost in the temple, "See how worried your father and I have been, looking for you.")

Homily Hints: The kids composed and presented a skit. In one scene, two girls are just watching TV. When Mom asks them to help with housework, they give her all sorts of phony excuses.

19

In the next scene the girls do help their Mom, and she rewards them with an ice cream cone. (The ice cream cone should be shown as a free gift, not something to be expected all the time.)

In a dialogue homily we talked about these two scenes and how they differ. We concluded that we should respect the mothers that God gave us.

God's love comes to us in many ways: through our mothers, through our offering ourselves in gifts of bread and wine.

Communion Hymn: "Immaculate Mary"

Recessional: "Thank You"

7. FRIENDSHIP

Background: At a parish liturgy the children respond readily to the theme of "friends." To emphasize the joy and outgoing nature of friendship, we passed out straw flowers to all people who came to Mass. The celebrant used a new vestment—a joyful one depicting children joining hands around the hem.

Opening Hymn: "We All Need One Another"

Introduction to the Mass (Read by child): Let us get ready for our celebration by remembering the joy and

20

happiness we find through friends. God, our Father, has given us many friends in the people and sometimes in the things around us. Jesus is a friend. He asks one thing of his friends: that they "love one another." Help us, Jesus, through this celebration, to find the many friends we have.

Penitential Rite:

Celebrant: For the times we insisted on our own way and didn't care about someone else's idea,
All: Lord, we are sorry.
Celebrant: For the times we turned away from other people, and the times we made fun of them,
All: Lord, we are sorry.
Celebrant: For the times we thought we were better than someone else,
All: Lord, we are sorry.
Celebrant: For the times we were mean to the people who love us most, our family,
All: Lord, we are sorry.
Celebrant: For refusing to be a friend to someone who needed us,
All: Lord, we are sorry.

Opening Prayer: Father, this day is your gift to us, filled with all the blessings of life which come from your hands. We have families and friends who love us, plenty to eat, good homes and a country where we all can go to school. What can we give you in return? You have asked us for one thing, that our love for each other be real. Help us to see that, behind the way a person dresses, looks and acts, there is someone a lot like us who wants to be our friend. Help us to reach out to each other in love and not to be afraid, for then we will find what you saw when you made us to be like you. Glory to you, Father, now and forever. Amen.

21

Reading I: Sirach: 6: 14-17 (adapted) (The great value of a friend)
Introduction to the reading: A good friend will not let us down; whoever finds one has found a real treasure. We cannot understand how wonderful a faithful friend can be. He is the joy of our life.

Whoever fears and trusts in the Lord makes real friends; if you are good, you will find a good friend.

Responsorial:
Lector: Whoever trusts in the Lord makes real friends.
All: Whoever trusts in the Lord makes real friends.
Lector: Let us care for each other as Jesus cares for us, and treat our friends as we wish to be treated.
All: Whoever trusts in the Lord makes real friends.
Lector: By listening carefully to others, we become closer to you, Lord.
All: Whoever trusts in the Lord makes real friends.
Lector: Let us use the gift of our voices to sing your praise and spread your words of love.
All: Trust in the Lord.

Alleluia Verse:
Lector: Alleluia, alleluia, alleluia.
All: Alleluia, alleluia, alleluia.
Lector: Sometimes you don't know who your friends are. Sometimes they are there all the time, but you walk right past them.
You don't notice that they like you in a special way.
All: Alleluia, alleluia, alleluia.

Reading II: John 15: 14-16 (adapted) (Jesus is our friend.)
Introduction to the Gospel: You are my friends if you do what I ask you. I shall not call you servant any more. From now on I'll call you my friend. A servant doesn't know his master's business. I will call you friends because I have told you everything I learned from my Father. What I ask you to do is love one another.

Homily Hints: "Once upon a time there was a seven-year-old boy who fell into a hole, and some other kids pulled him out. How can you tell they're friends? How do you want your friends to treat you?"

From these questions I continued: Friendship doubles our joy and divides our sorrow. We all know strangers; we each have buddies; and then there are friends. Like a rope for someone in a hole, friends can be counted on. We share secrets, laughs and tears with friends.

Jesus helps us to carry our joys and sorrows. When we're cold, he is too. When we're happy, so is he. Many of our friends move away; Jesus is our lifeline. We too must try to remain his friend, for "friendship doubles our joy and divides our grief." Our presence here today tells him we want him as a friend.

Prayers of the Faithful:

Lector: For people who understand, and people who sing, and people who are around when you need them most,
All: Thank you, Lord.
Lector: For all our friends with whom we share our secrets, laughs and tears,
All: Thank you, Lord.
Lector: For people who are different from us and proud of it; for people who have the courage to say what they believe,
All: Thank you, Lord.
Lector: For people who bring beauty into the world, and people who love, and people who do the best they can,
All: Thank you, Lord.
Lector: For all our friends of yesterday, today and tomorrow,
All: Thank you, Lord.

Offertory Hymn: "Take Our Bread"

Sign of Peace: Instead of a handshake, each person is asked to give his or her flower to someone else as a sign of friendship.

Communion Hymn: "Let Us Break Bread Together"

Recessional: "Peace, My Friends"

8. WATER

Background: Where does holy water come from? Not a bad question for a second grader! How is it made? To answer it I decided to bless holy water and use this sacramental in the liturgy.

Opening Hymn: "Joy Is Like the Rain" (one verse)

Reading I: Genesis 1:6-10 (The creation of water)

Responsorial: "Joy Is Like the Rain" (one verse)

Reading II: John 1: 29-34 (Jesus' Baptism)

Homily Hints: The homily was a blessing of holy water plus a sprinkling of the people.

Blessing of salt

Celebrant: O Lord, you have given us salt in order to taste things better; we pray for this salt that it may give its strength and seal to our ceremony today.

All: Blessed be the Lord forever.

Blessing of water

Celebrant: O Lord, creator of water, you have given us water to satisfy our thirst, to wash our bodies, and to cleanse. May this water be a sign of the inner cleansing that each of us is willing to undergo.

All: Lord, bless this water so that we who use it may be clean all over.

Celebrant pours salt into water in form of cross.

Celebrant: We mix salt and water in the name of the Father, and of the Son, and of the Holy Spirit.
All: Amen.
Celebrant: The Lord is with you.
All: And also with you.
Celebrant: Let us pray. Father, creator of all things and persons, we thank you for showing your love to us through these simple signs of water and salt. May we who touch this blessed water renew our desire to rise from our failures, to accept our limitations, and to be aware of your presence in our lives.
All: Amen, Lord. Both now and in the future.

The celebrant then puts blessed water into aspergil, asks all to kneel, and then does the customary "Asperges."

Offertory Procession: Bread and wine, grapes and wheat sheaves, plus other material gifts.

Communion Hymn: "Put Your Hand in the Hand"

Recessional: "The Living God"

9. GRATITUDE

Background: The theme of gratitude or thanks is often appropriate: at the beginning or end of summer, for national or family celebrations, for the start of the season, etc.

Opening Hymn: "Now Thank We All Our God"

Reading I: Ephesians 5: 19-20 ("Go on singing and chanting to the Lord in your hearts, so that always and everywhere you are giving thanks to God.")

Responsorial Psalm: Psalm 136
Cantor: His love is eternal.

All: His love is eternal.
Cantor: Give thanks to the Lord, because he is good.
All: His love is eternal.
Cantor: Give thanks to the greatest of all gods.
All: His love is eternal.
Cantor: Give thanks to the mightiest of all lords; he alone does great miracles.
All: His love is eternal.
Cantor: By his wisdom he made the heavens, he made the sun and the moon.
All: His love is eternal.
Cantor: Give thanks to the God of heaven.
All: His love is eternal.

Alleluia Verse:

Cantor: Alleluia, alleluia, alleluia.
All: Alleluia, alleluia, alleluia.
Cantor: Praise the Lord!
Praise God in his temple.
Praise his strength in heaven.
Praise him for the mighty things he has done.
Praise his supreme greatness.
All: Alleluia, alleluia, alleluia.

Reading II: Luke 10:25-37 (The Good Samaritan)

Homily Hints: Have the children identify with the priest, the Levite, and the Samaritan and share their feelings about the man attacked by robbers. Draw out parallels in our country and the world where this parable might be applicable.

Emphasize that Jesus is the Good Samaritan whom we meet today.

Holy, Holy, Holy: Sung.

Communion Hymn: "Whatsoever You Do"

Litany of Thanksgiving:

1) For giving yourself in Holy Communion,
Response: We thank you, God.

2) For our Church and school, so we can learn about God and the world, (Response)
3) For our pastors and teachers who help us more than we know, (Response)
4) For our parents who provide us with food, shelter, and clothing and many other things, (Response)
5) For our school where we learn and also enjoy each other, (Response)

Recessional: "Holy God, We Praise Thy Name"

10. FAITH IN THE ONE TRUE GOD

Background: One day at liturgy planning we discussed Comet Kohoutek. Our talk turned to the topic of the occult and how it manifests itself in our society today, e.g., *The Exorcist,* seances, ghosts, Ouija boards, black cats, broken mirrors. From these examples of superstitions and occultism we tried to recognize faith in the one true God.

Opening Hymn: "Come Holy Ghost" (two verses, especially the second verse which emphasizes "comforter.")

Reading I: Deuteronomy 18:9-14 (Occult practices are detestable before God.)

Responsorial: "You Are My People"

Alleluia Verse:
Lector: We will hear your Word, one in love, alleluia.
All: We will live your Word, one in love, alleluia.

Reading II: Luke 24:35-49 (Jesus appears to the apostles and gives them peace.)

Homily Hints: I put a ladder in the middle of the sanctuary and talked about the superstition: don't walk under a ladder. Who doesn't believe in this superstition? I called on a third grader, and asked him if he would walk under the ladder for us. He did; no problem.
    Faith is not like math where 2 + 2 might equal 4

and we're sure of it. Faith is trust in Jesus. Even
when the apostles saw Jesus as a ghost, they knew
he was real because they could believe him; he
was true to his promises. Faith also tells us that
Jesus is here too — among us, in his word, and in
Holy Communion.

Prayers of the Faithful:
Lector: For the times we turned from God to believe in
superstitions,
All: Lord, we are sorry.
Lector: For the times we have let horoscopes lead us instead
of allowing God to lead us,
All: Lord, we are sorry.
Lector: For the times that we have misguided our friends into
believing in superstitions,
All: Lord, we are sorry.

Offertory Hymn: "You Fill the Day"

Communion Hymn: "Spirit of God"

Recessional: "Put Your Hand in the Hand"

11. FEELINGS

Background: Children feel things more deeply than they are able
to verbalize. This liturgy approaches feelings positively —
especially the emotions of happiness and sadness — to see the
Christian dimension in them.

Opening Hymn: "The King of Glory" (The word of God is
something alive and active; it can judge the secret
emotions and thoughts.)

Reading I: Hebrews 4: 12-16 (Jesus understands us.)

Reading II: John 11:11-45 (Jesus brings his friend Lazarus back to
life.) For this reading, we used two sixth graders: a
narrator and one who spoke for Jesus.

Homily Hints: I began with an example from my own life, a time my
mother cried because she dropped her new iron. I

28

was sad about it, but I felt helpless to do anything for her. Such an incident speaks to children for they too can remember times their parents were happy or sad, times when they themselves were happy or sad.

The Gospel tells us that Jesus was very much like us — he laughed, he cried. But Jesus was aware of his feelings, because his feelings told him what a situation meant to him. Happy feelings tie us to Jesus' resurrection; sad feelings tie us to Jesus' death. In the Mass, we follow both Jesus' death and resurrection.

Offertory Hymn: "Love One Another"

Communion Hymn: "Prayer of St. Francis"

Recessional: "Spirit of God"

12. FISHING

Background: The children in our area love to go fishing — whether they catch anything or not. And so we chose the theme of fishing — of being caught by the Lord — as a springtime celebration. The boys and girls worked up a simple skit.

Explanation of Theme Before Mass: Matthew 13:47-51 ("The Kingdom of God is like a dragnet cast into the sea.")

Opening Hymn: "Michael, Row the Boat Ashore"

Reading I: Matthew 4:18-23 (Jesus selects fishermen as his first apostles, "Follow me and I will make you fishers of men.")

Responsorial: Psalm 118 (Paraphrase)
Lector: Oh, thank the Lord, for he's so good. His loving kindness is forever.
All: Oh, thank the Lord, for he's so good. His loving kindness is forever.
Lector: Let the teachers, priests and sisters say:

29

All: His loving kindness is forever.
Lector: Let all graduates say:
All: His loving kindness is forever.
Lector: In my hard times I prayed to the Lord.
All: And he answered me and rescued me.
Lector: The Lord is on my side.
All: He will help me. Amen. Alleluia.

Reading II: John 6:8-14 (Jesus multiplies the loaves and fishes for the crowd.)

Homily Hints: To illustrate the first reading, seven boys and girls and I put together a short skit.

The children were to one side of the sanctuary, and they held fishing poles, a net, strings and bucket. Here's the dialogue:

Celebrant: Boys and girls, where are you going?
Boy: We're going fishing.
Celebrant: (moving closer) Boys and girls, where are you going this morning?
Girl: Fishing!
Celebrant: If you follow me, we'll go fishing for the souls of men.
All: Yeah, let's go.
Celebrant: (raising hand) Whoever wants to follow, come on. (All walk down center aisle.)

The remainder of the homily could center in on the fishing experience, especially how fish fight back and struggle to free themselves.

We're like that too. We don't want the Lord to catch us, so sometimes we try to break away from him, too. Boys and girls, how can we follow Jesus better next week? (After Christmas, during Lent, this summer, etc.) How can we follow him better in the next few minutes?

Offertory Hymn: "Simple Gifts"

Communion Hymn: "Sunshine in My Soul"

Recessional: "The Mass Is Ended"

13. LOVE OF GOD IN MY HEART

Background: When I protested at a liturgy planning that the theme of "love, peace, helping, being kind" was too general, a little fourth grader responded, "We could show that people love differently, like two different size glasses that are both full."

Opening Hymn: "Sing"

Reading I: 1 Corinthians 12:31-13:12 (The greatest gift is love.)

Responsorial: "I Have Decided to Follow Jesus"

Reading II: John 13: 33-35 (Jesus gives a new commandment: to love.)

Homily Hints: Take two glasses of different sizes and one pitcher of Kool-Aid. Pour the same amount of Kool-Aid in each glass (the smaller one will look fuller.)

KOOLADE

Our hearts are only so big. We have to fill them up with something like the love of God. Our love leads to *actions*. The love in our hearts is reflected in love toward others. That's what Jesus did and continues to do now.

Prayers of the Faithful:
Lector: I pray that I may love you more, let us pray to the Lord.
All: Lord, hear our prayer.

Lector: I pray that all men may live in peace, let us pray to the Lord.

All: Lord, hear our prayer.

Lector: I pray that we may have the love of Jesus in our hearts, let us pray to the Lord.

All: Lord, hear our prayer.

Lector: I pray that we may share our toys with our brothers and sisters or friends that come over to play, let us pray to the Lord.

All: Lord, hear our prayer.

Communion Hymn: "This Little Light"

Recessional: "The Mass Is Ended"

14. FINGERPRINTS

Background: The students took their own fingerprints. They then made up stories, real or imaginary, of that fingerprint. The results were amusing, imaginative and beneficial. Here's an example from an 11-year-old fingerprint:

"The Fingerprint"

This fingerprint is known all over the world. It is the fingerprint of the late George Washington, our first President. He made it when he was 11 years old. Here is how he made it: George was writing a story about detectives. He wrote about fingerprints. His teacher had assigned it to him. He hated writing. So then he took some ink and made his fingerprint.

From this base we constructed our liturgy to explain that God has made us all the same (each of us has a fingerprint) and yet different (each fingerprint is different).

Opening Hymn: "He's Got the Whole World in His Hands"

Reading I: 1 Corinthians 12: 4-13 (The Holy Spirit gives us different gifts to serve the same Lord.)

Reading II: Matthew 20: 29-34 (Jesus cures the two blind men of

Jericho; he accepts everybody, no matter who they are, because each is important.)

Homily Hints: I asked the kids to look at the giant "fingerprint poster" we had taped to the altar. Then I asked them to look at their own thumbprint and to compare how theirs was similar/different than the person's next to them. God has made us different and yet the same. We're special. He's going to come to us soon.

Offertory Hymn: "Of My Hands"

Recessional: "Be a New Man"

15. NEWS

Background: Children see TV constantly, read papers, and often have opinions on current events. The students at our school even put out a school newspaper, the *Good News*.

Opening Hymn: "Go Tell It on the Mountain"

Reading I: Romans 8: 26-31 (All that happens is working for our good.)

Responsorial: "Go Tell It on the Mountain" (a second time)

Reading II: John 20: 1-9 (Mary of Magdala, Simon Peter and John discover the empty tomb and give a witness account of faith in Jesus' resurrection.)

Homily Hints: If we were to take an imaginary trip from the church to the local movie theatre, we'd meet both good and bad "news" along the way. Ask the kids for examples of each. Bad news might be: a dog killed on the street, water in basements after floods, getting lost along the way. Good news might be: singing while walking, no mud puddles, green lights.
    Jesus helps us accept both good and bad news.

Offertory Hymn: "They'll Know We Are Christians"

Sign of Peace: Say to one another: "Go tell the good news."

Communion Hymn: "Battle Hymn of the Republic"

Recessional: "Allelu, Allelu"

16. BROTHERHOOD

Background: Primary age school children were the participants in the liturgy which included a simple five-minute play. The liturgy and the play highlight the theme of "brotherhood," a theme the students can prepare for weeks in advance by concentrating on the play, *The Three Little Butterfly Brothers.* This liturgy took place in church, and the sanctuary became the stage for the play.

Opening Hymn: "Raise Your Hands"

Apology Time: Primary children appreciate the word "apology" rather than "penitential" or "purification." The leader can direct the group to apologize to one another and to God for wrongs done to one's brothers and sisters.

Reading I: I John 2: 9-11 ("Anyone who claims to be in the light but hates his brother is still in the dark.")

Response: Sing Alleluia.

Reading II: John 15: 12-17 ("What I command you is to love one another.")

Homily Hints: Play — *The Three Little Butterfly Brothers* This play is simple enough for young primary children but it does need preparation. The children can memorize their parts; and if the teacher can make the butterfly wings, rain drops, clouds, sun and flowers, the children watching will be able to follow the play easier.

The Three Little Butterfly Brothers
(taken from *Joy* magazine, April-May, 1972)
Introduction (by an adult): Hello, everybody, we are going to act

34

out the story of *The Three Little Butterfly Brothers* for you. Please use your imagination as you listen. Make believe that you are in a beautiful garden (indicate real flowers). When you look at the people in the play, don't see boys and girls you know. Make believe that you see butterflies (indicate butterflies), and a lily, a tulip, and the sun (indicate each in turn). Something happens to the butterflies — something both sad and happy. And it's something that might happen to us, too. (Pause) Now, the storyteller is ready. Let's listen. (All the characters except the lily and tulip leave the stage. Storyteller stands at right or left of stage area.)

Storyteller: Once there were three little butterfly brothers. One was yellow . . . (Yellow butterfly comes out and bows.)

Storyteller: One was white . . . (White butterfly comes out and bows.)

Storyteller: And one was red. (Red butterfly comes out and bows.)

Storyteller: Every day when the sun was shining, the butterfly brothers went to play in the garden. (Sun comes out and stands in middle, back stage. Butterflies flutter and fly among the flowers.)

Storyteller: One day, dark clouds covered the sun. (Clouds cover the sun.)

Storyteller: And it began to rain. (Two rains come in and move arms gently up and down to indicate rain.)

White Butterfly: My wings are getting wet!

Yellow Butterfly: Let's fly away home! (Butterflies fly to a make-believe home and try to open the door. They tug and pull and can't get it open.)

Red Butterfly: The door is locked.

White Butterfly: The key is gone.

Yellow Butterfly: We can't get in.

Storyteller: It began to rain harder. (Two more rains come in and stand with others, moving arms.)

Storyteller: The butterfly brothers got wetter and wetter. (Butterflies flutter slowly toward the red tulip.)

White Butterfly: Look at this beautiful red and yellow tulip.

Red Butterfly: It looks big enough for all three of us.

Three Butterflies: Friend Tulip, please open your flower cup and let us come in out of the rain.

Tulip: The red and yellow butterflies are like me, so they may come

35

in. But the white one may not come in. (The white butterfly flutters a little ways away. The red and yellow butterflies go after him and stand with him.)

Red Butterfly: If our white brother may not come in, we will not come in.

Yellow Butterfly: We want to stay together.

Storyteller: It rained harder and harder. (More rains come in.)

Storyteller: The three butterfly brothers got very wet. They looked for another place big enough to keep three little butterflies out of the rain. (The three butterflies flutter slowly to the white lily.)

Red Butterfly: Good Lily, let us come in, out of the rain.

White Butterfly: We are very wet.

Lily: The white butterfly is like me, so he may come in. But the red and yellow butterflies may not come in. (The red and yellow butterflies begin to flutter away, and the white goes after them.)

White Butterfly: If my red and yellow brothers may not come in, I will not come in. We want to stay together. (The butterflies huddle together in the middle of the stage, moving their wings only a little.)

Yellow Butterfly: I can hardly fly.

Red Butterfly: I am so cold.

White Butterfly: No one will help us.

Storyteller: Up in the sky, the sun was shining behind the rain clouds. He had heard everything.

Sun's Voice: The three little butterfly brothers love each other and they have stayed together, in spite of the rain. I will help them. (The sun moves forward, and the clouds lower, so his shining face can be seen.)

Sun: Rain, stop! (Rain stops.)

Sun: Go away, clouds! (Sun chases clouds and rain out.)

Sun: Now I will shine on the butterflies and make them warm and dry. (Sun moves close to the butterflies and they begin to move a little.)

White Butterfly: I feel warm and my wings are almost dry. Wake up, brothers!

Yellow Butterfly: The sun has chased away the rain.

Red Butterfly: Let us play and dance. (The butterflies dance and flutter among the flowers.)

Storyteller: The butterfly brothers played in the garden until the

36

sun went down . . . (Sun goes out.)
Red Butterfly: Look! (Red Butterfly points off stage. The other butterflies look.)
White Butterfly: The door of our house is open.
Red Butterfly: The light is shining! We can go home together! (The butterflies put their arms around each other and fly home together. Or, they sing a familiar song, such as "Here We Are," and all the cast join in.)

The End

By Agnes Lawless, copyright© 1972, *Joy* Level Three Teacher Guide. Winston Press, Minneapolis, Minn. 55403. Used with permission. All rights reserved. *The Three Little Butterfly Brothers* is from *Deutches Drittes Lesebuch.* W.H. Weick, C. Grebner.

The celebrant can then relate the play to our lives. Leading questions might be: What happened? Are you happy? Sad? How is this play true for our lives? Does this play ask us to take care of one another?
Jesus is our brother and we remember in this Mass the important things he did for us.

Offertory Hymn: "She's Just an Old Stump"

Acclamation: "Christ Has Died, Alleluia"

Sign of Peace: "Prayer of St. Francis"

Recessional: "To Be a Friend"

17. PEACE

Background: This liturgy on peace coincided with the 1973 Vietnam cease-fire, but it is applicable to the general theme of peace. We used it as a children's liturgy at a regularly scheduled parish Mass, with the children taking the main parts. A burlap and felt banner showing hands of all colors stretching across a globe was hung in front of the altar.

Opening Hymn: "Let There Be Peace on Earth"

Penitential Rite:

> Lector: We are sorry for the times we argued with others because we did not trust them.
>
> All: Lord, make me an instrument of your peace.
>
> Celebrant: Happy are those who strive for peace; they shall be called the sons of God.
>
> Lector: We are sorry for the times when we lost our tempers with others and thus hurt their feelings.
>
> All: Lord, make me an instrument of your peace.
>
> Celebrant: Happy are those who strive for peace; they will be called sons of God.
>
> Lector: We are sorry for the times when our jealousy of others made us steal things so that we could be like them.
>
> All: Lord, make me an instrument of your peace.
>
> Celebrant: Happy are those who strive for peace; they shall be called the sons of God.

Reading I: Ephesians 2: 14 and 16 ("For he is the peace between us.")

Responsorial Psalm:

> Lector: Lord, make us loving tools of your peace and goodness.
>
> All: Lord, make us loving tools of your peace and goodness.
>
> Lector: All those who work for peace are happy; God will call them his sons.
>
> All: Lord, make us loving tools of your peace and goodness.
>
> Lector: To live in peace we should try to see the good in people, not the bad.
>
> All: Lord, make us loving tools of your peace and goodness.
>
> Lector: Christ's blessings be fulfilled in us, for blessed are the peacemakers; they shall be called the children of God.
>
> All: Lord, make us loving tools of your peace and goodness.

Reading II: Isaiah 61: 1-8

Reading III: John 14: 27-29 (Jesus gives us peace, "My own peace I give you.")

Homily Hints: This homily tried to make the children and adults aware of how we are not peacemakers but make and glorify war and violence in our own lives. What we do is a microcosm of what nations do.

I mentioned movies in town and even television cartoons ("George of the Jungle" and "Road-Runner") that were quite violent. I quoted reports of driving deaths, crimes and war casualties. Then I emphasized specific examples of how Jesus brings us peace of mind and heart.

Let's take hold of Jesus' gift of peace.

Offertory Hymn: "Let Us Break Bread Together"

Sign of Peace: Children who composed the liturgy extend the sign of peace to the congregation after having received it from the celebrant.

Communion Hymn: "Prayer for Peace"

Recessional: "Let There Be Peace on Earth"

18. A BIRTHDAY: NEW LIFE

Background: Even though each of us has a birthday which we celebrate with parties and games, we seldom take time out to celebrate our birthdays in a liturgical way. This liturgy speaks of the new life that Jesus brings into our lives.

Opening Hymn: "Be a New Man"

Opening Prayer: Lord, Father, every year we have a chance to be happy again when we celebrate our birthdays. Thanks for my birthday, Lord, for it gives me a chance to breathe more fresh air, make new friends, enjoy the sun — and most of all, to thank you for giving all those things to me. We say, "Thanks," through Christ our Lord.

Reading I: Luke 8: 49-56 (Jairus' daughter is raised to life.)

Responsorial:

Left side: Bless my eyes, Lord. Help me to see you in the world and in people I meet.

Right side: Bless my ears, Lord. Help me to hear your voice in the sounds around me.

Left side: Bless my lips, Lord. Help me to use my power of speech to proclaim your glory.

Right side: Bless my hands, Lord. Help me to use these hands to build your kindgom on this earth.

Reading II: Luke 19: 1-10 (This story about the meeting of Zacchaeus and Jesus offers a good chance for a three part dialogue: Jesus, narrator and Zacchaeus.)

Homily Hints: A birthday cake that the children can share later is a good visual aid. Ask the students who has had a birthday this month. This week. Ask them about the birth of a younger brother or sister.

Inviting Jesus into their hearts *right now* as Zacchaeus did is a birth of new life. When Jesus comes, we have life from that moment.

Offertory Hymn: "Put Your Hand in the Hand"

Our Father: Sung

Sign of Peace: Greet one another with "Smile, God loves you" or the children can pass out "happy face" badges that they made earlier with the phrase, "Smile, God loves you."

Communion Hymn: "Spirit of God"

Recessional: "The Mass Is Ended"

19. HANDS

Background: Many expressions that include the word "hand" demonstrate the use of the hands when people give to each other, help each other, or show friendship: "helping hand," "hand-out," "join hands," "lend a hand," "handshake," "hand-in-hand." Hands are associated with creation — mothers cook using their hands; fathers build (and vice versa sometimes). Hands are used especially to touch and pet when a parent soothes a child or gives a back rub.

The work to be done now (Christ's work) must be ours — we have to do what his hands would do.

Opening Hymn: "Knock on Any Door" (*Joy* magazine, 3rd grade ed., Spring, '74)

Penitential Rite:
    Celebrant: For the times we didn't lend a helping hand to someone who needed us,
    All: Lord, we are sorry.
    Celebrant: For the times we didn't show love for others by reaching out our hands in forgiveness,
    All: Lord, we are sorry.
    Celebrant: For the times we used our hands to hurt instead of help,
    All: Lord, we are sorry.

Reading I: Psalm 95: 4-5,7 (adapted) (God makes us and cares for us, "We are the people of his pasture, and the sheep of his hand.")

Responsorial: Job 10: 8-9,11-12 (adapted) ("Your own hands shaped me, modeled me.")
    Lector: Your hands have formed me the way I am.
    All: Your hands have formed me the way I am.
    Lector: You have made me as clay, and I will someday be dust again.

All: Your hands have formed me the way I am.
Lector: You have put on me clothes of skin and flesh. You fashioned me of bone and sinew.
All: Your hands have formed me the way I am.
Lector: You have given me life and mercy; your being with me has kept me alive.
All: Your hands have formed me the way I am.
Lector: Although you don't always show yourself to me, I know that you remember me.
All: Your hands have formed me the way I am.

Alleluia Verse: "Alleluia! We Will Hear Your Word"

Reading III: Mark 7: 32-35 (Jesus heals a deaf mute.)

Homily Hints: "Let's look at our hands. What do little boys/girls, moms/dads do with their hands? I then produced a tube of Play Doh and fashioned it into a small stick man. Hands hurt/help, create/destroy things and persons.

Just as Jesus healed, we too can heal and become his hands in our world.

Prayers of the Faithful:
Lector: For children, who have happy, hoping hands,
All: We thank you, Lord.
Lector: For mothers, who have soft, tender hands,
All: We thank you, Lord.
Lector: For fathers, who have strong, caring hands,
All: We thank you, Lord.
Lector: For priests, who have blessed, helping hands,
All: We thank you, Lord.
Lector: For this creation, where in all the works of your hands we find traces of love,
All: We thank you, Lord.

Offertory Hymn: "Of My Hands"

Sign of Peace: A reference to joining hands.

Communion Hymn: "He's Got the Whole World in His Hands"

Recessional: "Knock on Any Door"

20. COMMUNICATION

Background: We planned for this liturgy by role-playing a family situation in which parent and child get angry at one another and miss the communication. This role-playing led to the theme of communication and the choosing of readings from the Bible concerning anger.

Opening Hymn: "Here We Are" (Students all join hands.)

Penitential Rite:
> Lector: We are sorry for hurting people by calling them names or telling them to shut up.
> All: Lord, we are sorry.
> Lector: We do not always listen to the other person when we are angry.
> All: Lord, we are sorry.
> Lector: We don't always give our parents a chance, and we get angry at them for nothing.
> All: Lord, we are sorry.

Reading I: Acts 4: 8-12 (Peter relays Good News about the power of Jesus.)

Responsorial: "Sing Praise to the Lord" (just chorus)

Reading II: Luke 19: 46-48 (Jesus teaches in the temple, "The people as a whole hung on his words.")

Homily Hints: I used hand gestures to describe good and bad communication: my two index fingers together in front of my face as an example of good communication; my index fingers bypassing each other as an indication of poor or missed communication. In our Christian lives we have to be consistent — our words must agree with our actions for good communications to occur.

Jesus not only *said* he would be willing to suffer, but he actually *did* undergo sufferings. His communication with the Father was genuine and honest. That's what the Mass is all about.

Recessional: "The Mass Is Ended"

21. IT'S WHAT'S ON THE INSIDE
THAT COUNTS

Background: While talking about various topics with a group of sixth graders, someone commented, "Father, it's what's on the inside of us that counts." This phrase became the theme for a liturgy. We put it into print on a large poster made by the class.

Opening Hymn: "God Made Us All"

Reading I: Colossians 3:11-17 (We treat others according to what is in our hearts, "Let the peace of Christ rule in your hearts.")

Reading II: Matthew 23 (Jesus' words against the hypocrisy of the Pharisees.)

Homily Hints: (1) Use a halloween mask to bring out the theme of the Mass. Ask the children how in other ways boys and girls act differently on the outside from what they feel on the inside. Our Christian purpose is harmony between outside and inside.

(2) Have three children dress up in costumes that do not give away their identity. Then ask each dressed up person a series of questions:
What is your favorite hobby?
Who is your best friend?
What subject do you like best?
The "inside" of the person should emerge, and you can continue to draw out the significance of the scriptural readings.
The Liturgy of the Eucharist is the "inside" of Jesus speaking to us.

Recessional: "Everything Is Beautiful"

22. KINGDOM OF GOD

Background: This liturgy was for a Mexican-American group of primary students. Often theological jargon and phrases like

"Kingdom of God" are difficult for children. This liturgy attempts to visualize, to make flesh, the reality "Kingdom of God" for children. For this liturgy, you will need a number of large cardboard boxes.

Introduction: Draw attention to cardboard boxes.

Opening Hymn: "The Kingdom of God" (3 verses)

Penitential Rite: "Lord Have Mercy" (sung)

Reading I: 1 Corinthians 12:14-21;26-28 ("Now you together are Christ's body; but each of you is a different part of it.")

Responsorial: "The Kingdom of God" (fourth verse)

Reading II: Matthew 13:31-32 ("The Kingdom of Heaven is like a mustard seed.")

Homily Hints: Select a boy and girl to help you. Place them in front and then proceed to wall them off from other children by placing boxes in front of them, thus hiding them from others. While building the wall, label each box with something we do wrong to hurt the "one body of Christ." (Ask students for their suggestions too.) Then, take wall apart by labeling each box with a positive way we can treat one another.

Emphasize the "Kingdom of God" is God's life among us which we can either foster and build up or retard by creating barriers. The more the children are involved in the homily, the more eager they are to learn and absorb the lesson.

The remainder of the Mass is our chance to be "open" with Jesus and invite him into our hearts.

Offertory Hymn: "Simple Gifts" with a procession.

Communion Hymn: "I've Got Peace Like a River"

Recessional: "Magical Box"

23. LISTENING

Background: You've heard parents say, "I say something to my kid, and it goes in one ear and out the other." So we decided to have a liturgy on listening.

Opening Hymn: "The King of Glory"

Reading I: Romans 10:14-16 ("Not everyone, of course, listens to the Good News.")

Reading II: John 8:43-47 ("A child of God listens to the words of God.")

Homily Hints: There's a difference between *hearing* (in one ear and out the other) and *listening* (paying attention to and acting on what is said). I used hand gestures to indicate "hearing" (right index finger pointing to right ear/left thumb pointing away from left ear) and "listening" (both index fingers pointing to respective ears). We hear "go take a bath," but we don't listen. We hear "time for bed," but don't listen.

When it comes to God, we must *listen* to both his outer Word (Bible reading, liturgical services) and his inner Word (inner impulses like conscience, awareness of his presence).

Offertory Hymn: "Hear, O Lord"

Communion Hymn: "Sons of God"

Recessional: "Whatsoever You Do"

24. BE PREPARED

Background: The scout motto is "Be Prepared" — almost a way of approaching all experiences in life. We can be prepared to assist a grandparent across the room, or be prepared to catch a fly ball in left field. Children can also "be prepared" for God, be aware of where he breaks into their lives.

Opening Hymn: "Isn't the Love of Jesus Something"

Readings: Matthew 25: 1-13 (The story of the 10 bridesmaids)
Matthew 25: 31-46 (The Last Judgment)
(alternates)
Matthew 13 (The parable of the Good Seed)
Matthew 19: 13-15 (Jesus and little children)
Matthew 13: 44-51 (The Kingdom of Heaven discovery parables — the treasure, a fine pearl, a dragnet)

Homily Hints: We prepare ourselves, get ourselves alert and tuned up, for a vacation, a soft ball game, a test, a trip to the fair or circus. We expect great things. In our life with God, we can be prepared to meet him in many forms: in praying, in doing good works, in being happy, in loving others, in being strong while sick.
Be prepared for Jesus to be with us. We can discover him everywhere, especially here at the Eucharist when we are attentive to the offering of bread and wine and the coming of Jesus in Holy Communion.

Prayers of the Faithful: Initial prayers by celebrant and then spontaneous prayers by children and teachers.

Offertory Hymn: "All That I Am"

Our Father: Sung.

47

Sign of Peace: Creativity during this portion of the Mass is important. A suggestion: touch shoulder of boy/girl next to you and say "have a nice day."

Communion Hymn: "Kum Ba Ya"

Recessional: "Shout From the Highest Mountain"

II School Situations

25. HELLO

Background: When we get up grumpy, a cheerful "hello" is a beginning of a brighter day. When we move into a new place, we're scared of meeting new children until one says hello. Hello is the opposite of goodbye, a word that often hurts people when we use it to keep other boys and girls from playing in our games or when we translate goodbye into action by fighting with a friend. At the end of the school year, we don't say "goodbye" but "hello" because Jesus is not abandoning us. He will be with us throughout the summer.

Although this liturgy relates well to the beginning of a school year or a religious education program, it has possibilities for the close of the school year too. Students can stand at the entrance way or doors and greet students with "hello" before liturgy.

Opening Hymn: Recorded song "Hello" (Saying hello is a beginning.)

Introduction: Theme introduced by one of the students.

Penitential rite: Celebrant or students can bring out examples of when we hurt others through our "goodbyes."

Opening Prayer: Father, on Pentecost you sent the Holy Spirit into our lives to say "hello" to us. Help us to love others by saying "hello" to them. Through Christ our brother. Amen.

Reading I: Mark 13: 34-37 (Watch for my return.)

Alleluia verse: Alleluia. I will come at evening, at midnight, early dawn, or at daybreak. Await my return. Alleluia.

Reading II: John 14:15-19 ("I shall ask the Father and he will give you another advocate to be with you forever, the Spirit of truth.")

Homily Hints: To create a human basis for the "hello" theme, remind the students of how they answer the telephone; of how they greet parents, relatives and friends who live far away; of the "hello" they received walking in for liturgy.

Now make use of what I call a "hello box." (All you need is a cardboard box in which you put a plaque that says HELLO on it — but don't let the students see what is in the box.)

Have different classes or groups of children shout "hello" to you and tell them you will gather their hello's into your box. After they have all shouted hello, show them the plaque — their hello's have become something visible and tangible. The plaque may now be placed on the altar for the Liturgy of the Eucharist.

Just as our "hello" became visible in the plaque, so also Jesus' promise of a helper and comforter became visible in the sending of the Spirit. The Spirit is Jesus' "hello" which comes to us in listening to the Word of God and in the breaking of the bread.

Offertory Hymn: "Take Our Bread"

Great Amen: Sung to the melody from "Lilies of the Field"

Recessional: "My Lord Will Come Again"

26. FRIENDS

Background: The intermediate grades composed this liturgy on friendship. It's a popular theme, adaptable to any season or circumstance. This Eucharist could be in the classroom itself.

Opening Hymn: "Let There Be Peace on Earth"

Reading I: Sirach 6:5-17 ("A faithful friend is a sure shelter.")

Reading II: John 15:12-17 ("I call you friends because I have made known to you everything I have learned from my Father.")

Homily Hints: (1) Start a dialogue homily with the children with questions like: What are examples of friendship? What are ways we don't show friendship?

(2) Select two children and have them role-play a

friendly and a hostile situation from their lives.
We have a constant friend in Jesus who again tells us that we are important.

Offertory Hymn: "Everything Is Beautiful"

Our Father: Sung to a known melody.

Communion Hymn: "Spirit of God"

Recessional: "He's Got the Whole World in His Hands"

27. THINK AHEAD

Background: Christmas vacation is great, but it's so difficult to come back to school after the new year. In this liturgy we looked back over Christmas and thought ahead — prepared — for the next Christmas. We prepare for many things — school, birthday parties, trips, etc. We also prepare our hearts for Jesus during this year.

Opening Hymn: "Joy to the World"

Reading I: Matthew 22:1-10 (The parable of the wedding feast)

Alleluia: Sung.

Reading II: Matthew 25:1-13 (The parable of the 10 bridesmaids, "So stay awake because you do not know, either the day or the hour.)

Homily Hints: It's the new year, so let's think back over the past Christmas. What did you *like* about Christmas this past year? (responses from children). What did you *not like* about it? (responses from children). How do you want to plan ahead or be prepared for Christmas next year?
How can we begin now in this time given to us?

Offertory Hymn: "All That I Am"

Communion Hymn: "Sons of God"

Recessional: "Hark, the Herald Angels Sing"

28. CHEATING

Background: In talking with the school children, I discovered that some of them cheated and that the others knew about the cheating and who was doing it. Everyone had feelings about cheating and cheaters.

Opening Hymn: "All the Earth Proclaim the Lord"

Reading I: Acts 5:1-11 (Ananias and his wife Sapphira try to cheat the early Church.)

Reading II: II Timothy 2:1-7 (Christians, like athletes, must practice discipline, "Or take an athlete — he cannot win any crown unless he has kept all the rules of the contest.")

Reading III: Luke 18:18-21 (Jesus insists that following the commandments is necessary for eternal life, "You know the commandments . . .")

Homily Hints: The important thing in most games is not whether you win or lose but how you play the game. A good person, just like a good baseball player, needs the help of certain rules. A good person, a good player, follows the rules and thus does not need to cheat.

When Jesus died, it seemed like he "lost"; but he really "won." He did what his Father asked him to do. As we continue this Mass, let's try to follow Jesus' example.

Offertory Hymn: "All That I Am"

Communion Hymn: "Seek Ye First"

Recessional: "Come Away"

29. WEEKEND HAPPENINGS

Background: The weekend is always fresh in the students' minds. Why not use that freshness and build a theme around those actions? Let's see how our lives fit in with Jesus' life.

Opening Hymn: "Spirit of God" (first verse, chorus)

Reading I: I John 4:4-11 ("Let us love one another since love comes from God.")

Responsorial: "Spirit of God" (second verse, chorus.)

Reading II: John 1:5-14 (His life is our light, "The Word was the true light that enlightens all men; and he was coming into the world.")

Homily Hints: Iris were in bloom at the time, and I presented the students with one live one and one dead one. The live one represented my life when Jesus is a part of my weekend experiences; the dead one when I left Jesus out of the weekend.

We can compare the bloom of a flower to Jesus' resurrection as we recall it in the Mass.

Prayer Over the Gifts: Lord, we give to you our gifts of bread and wine. These gifts are the signs of the weekend experiences I had. Change these gifts, Lord, and me too.

Communion Hymn: "Be a New Man"

Recessional: "Allelu, Allelu"

30. ALL PEOPLE ARE DIFFERENT

Background: Classes often look upon themselves as self-contained and complete until someone new moves into town and joins that class. This liturgy helps us give that new person a chance to become part of the group. We need to recognize that all people are different and that's okay.

Opening Hymn: "Everything Is Beautiful"
(Alternate between kids singing the chorus and a song leader reading the verses.)

Reading I: Ephesians 4:9-13 (We are parts of the one body, "The saints together make a unity in the work of service, building up the Body of Christ.")

Reading II: 1 Peter 4:7-11 ("Each of you has received a special grace.")

Reading III: Matthew 5:13-16 ("You are the salt of the earth . . . You are the light of the world.")

Homily Hints: "Kids, give me one fact about yourself, something that describes you." After discussing these self-descriptions, I showed the kids two different doughnuts. We saw how each doughnut was different yet special.
Jesus has accepted us; we too ought to love one another.

Our Father: Sung.

Communion Hymn: "This Little Light"

Recessional: "What Color Is God's Skin?"

31. COMPARISONS

Background: The kids have one word for report card time — "Yuk." Some kids dread receiving the cards; and when they do receive them, they compare their grades. This liturgy grew out of a discussion on report cards just after they were given out at school.

Procession: Have the children bring in two huge report card posters, one showing good grades, the other poor grades.

Opening Hymn: "It's a Long Road to Freedom"

Reading I: Philippians 3:4-10 (Externals are not important, "if I can have Christ and be given a place in him.")

Responsorial Hymn: "Rejoice in the Lord Always"

Reading II: Colossians 3:12-17 (Love binds all things together in unity.)

Reading III: John 15:12-15 ("I call you friends.")

Homily Hints: I held up each report card poster and asked the children, "Would you show this report card to others?" The card with the poor grades *embarrassed* the kids; they felt others would *laugh* at them, and that their poor grades would be known all over the school.

Some students are usually the first ones finished on a test, the higher scorers on achievement tests. Good marks often bring praise (and occasionally money) while poor marks bring frowns and scoldings.

Isn't it great that we don't have to perform for the Lord since he loves us no matter what grades we get! We don't have to get an "A" for God to love us.

Offertory Hymn: "Let Us Break Bread Together"

Communion Hymn: "Joy Is Like the Rain"

Recessional: "Be a New Man"

32. SING *YOUR* SONG

Background: As a closing Mass for the CCD children, we wanted a theme that would acknowledge the work done during the year and encourage the children for the summer and the next fall's religion classes. We hit on the theme that each of us has a special song to sing; and using Carpenters' song, "Sing," we had our liturgy.

Opening Hymn: "Sing" by Carpenters

Reading I: Romans 12:1-12 ("Our gifts differ according to the grace given us.")

Responsorial Psalm: (From *Come Out,* by Sisters Elizabeth Blandford and Janet Marie Bucher. Copyright ©1971, World Library Publications.)

Lector: God gave me feet to dance with.
All: I'm specially made to be me.
Lector: God gave me eyes to see with.
All: I'm specially made to be me.
Lector: God gave me a voice to speak with.
All: I'm specially made to be me.
Lector: God gave me a nose to smell a rose.
All: I'm specially made to be me.
Lector: God gave me knees to kneel on.
All: I'm specially made to be me.
Lector: God gave me hair to keep my head warm.
All: I'm specially made to be me.
Lector: God gave me brains to think with.
All: I'm specially made to be me.
Lector: God gave me a heart to love with.
All: I'm specially made to be me.

Reading II: Matthew 5:6-10 (adapted) (The Beatitudes)

One day Jesus went up on a hillside with his disciples. He sat down and taught them there. This is what he said:

Happy are people who discover that they need God; they will be with God forever.

Happy are those who know what sadness means; God will comfort them.

Happy are people who are gentle; they will receive what God has promised.

Happy are those who want with all their heart to do what is right; God will fill them with love.

Happy are those who are kind; they will receive kindness.

Happy are those who let their hearts be filled with God's love; they will see God.

Happy are those who work for peace; God will call them his children.

Happy are people who suffer because they do what is right; heaven belongs to them!

Homily Hints: In the game of "Tag" we touch someone and say "you're it." Each of us has a special song — your song, you're it. What can you do well? Ride a bike? Draw? Play the piano? Eat a banana split? Did you make your First Communion this year?

Continue through the summer to learn your song and to make it last your whole life long.

At Mass, Jesus touches us to tell us it's okay to sing our special song. He likes us and takes this time to tell us so.

Prayers of Faithful:

Lector: Help us to see that each of us is special.

All: Lord, hear our prayer,

Lector: Give each of us the courage to live in peace with our brothers and sisters.

All: Lord, hear our prayer.

Lector: Help each of us to see our own special abilities and not be ashamed of them.

All: Lord, hear our prayer.

Lector: Help us not to give up when many things are going wrong.

All: Lord, hear our prayer.

Lector: Help us to keep the love song for Jesus going on and on.

All: Lord, hear our prayer.

Offertory Hymn: "Take Our Bread"

Communion Hymn: "Everything Is Beautiful"

Recessional: "Sing"

33. HAVE A SABBATH SUMMER

Background: This liturgy culminated our religious education classes for the year. The theme emphasizes that we should remember the Lord throughout the summer, that our rest should give us time to be aware of all that God does for us.

Opening Hymn: "Enter, Rejoice and Come in"

Penitential Rite:
Celebrant: For the times we wouldn't let others play with us,
All: We are sorry, Lord.
Celebrant: For the times we wouldn't be a friend to someone who needed us,
All: We are sorry, Lord.
Celebrant: For the times we didn't listen to our parents and teachers,
All: We are sorry, Lord.
Celebrant: For the times we had a wonderful day or a special friend or a great surprise, and we forgot to thank you,
All: We are sorry, Lord.

Reading I: Genesis 2:2-3 ("He rested on the seventh day . . . God blessed the seventh day and made it holy.")

Responsorial:
Right side of church: Bless my eyes, Lord. Help me to see you in the world and in the people I meet.

Left side of church: Bless my ears, Lord. Help me to hear your voice in the sounds around me.

Right side of church: Bless my lips, Lord. Help me to use my power of speech to glorify you.

Left side of church: Bless my hands, Lord. Help me to use these hands to build your kingdom on this earth.

Reading II: Luke 6:43-45 ("A good man draws what is good from the store of goodness in his heart.")

Homily Hints: I asked the left side of church to think back for a happy experience during the past school year; the right side was to remember a sad event. I asked the children then to think of how God might touch them during the first part of the summer.

Sabbath summer is the opportunity to think back, to remember what the Lord has done for us. Just as we practice ball or learn how to ride a bike, we also need to practice our Sabbath summer.

This Eucharist helps us to remember the happy and sad events in Jesus' life.

Prayers of the Faithful:

Lector: Help us to remember you are with us during our summer fun.

All: Lord, hear our prayer.

Lector: Help each of us to see our own special abilities and not be ashamed of them.

All: Lord, hear our prayer.

Lector: Help us remember to ask you for help when we are unhappy or afraid.

All: Lord, hear our prayer.

Lector: Bless those people who are trying to help us learn more about you.

All: Lord, hear our prayer.

Offertory Hymn: "All That I Am"

Communion Hymn: "Gonna Sing, My Lord"

Recessional: "Sing" (by Carpenters)

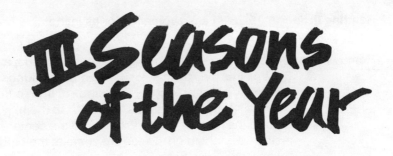

III Seasons of the Year

34. THE JESSE TREE

Background: We used this Advent liturgy to emphasize the waiting and preparation of the world for the coming of Jesus. It uses the story and symbols of the Jesse Tree and highlights the deep Jewish roots of our religion. We presented this liturgy at a parish liturgy.

Opening Hymn: "Jesse Tree Song"

Reading I: Isaiah 11:1,6-7 ("A shoot springs from the stock of Jesse.")

Response: All: Hark the word by Christmas spoken
Let the sword of war be broken,
Let the wrath of battle cease.
Christmas has no word but peace.

Reading II: John 1:19-23 ("I am a voice that cries in the wilderness.")

Homily Hints: Christmas tree lights make an excellent visual aid. For this liturgy, I tried to visualize different kinds of people by pointing out various kinds of light bulbs.

Get a string of Christmas lights. Wrap them around the lecturn or carry them into the center aisle — turn them on. These are some of the bulb-symbols you can have:

(1) Solid color, non-blinking: this bulb represents all people who eagerly awaited the Savior. They're turned on to listening and finding Jesus.

(2) Solid color, blinking: this periodic blinker is like many people who get turned on to Jesus but begin to lose interest. Sometimes they're on — and sometimes off.

(3) A burned-out bulb: represents people who turn their backs on Jesus.

During the remainder of the Mass and this Advent, let's be like these solid color, non-blinking bulbs as we await Jesus in the Eucharist and in his coming at Christmas.

Offertory Hymn: "O Come, Little Children"

Preface: After the Preface responses, we have the Jesse Tree ceremony. Children will place on the Jesse tree the symbols which represent people who waited for the Savior. After the words, "waiting for the Savior," please answer, "We are waiting, too, O Lord."

(1) Adam and Eve took a bite of the forbidden apple. Then they waited for the Savior. (Response)

(2) Noah floated in the Ark, waiting for the Savior. (Response)

(3) Abraham walked to the promised land. He was waiting for the Savior. (Response)

(4) Jacob wrestled with an angel while he waited for the Savior. (Response)

(5)   Moses saw God in the burning bush; he was waiting for the Savior. (Response)

(6)   Jesse was the father of kings, but he waited for the Savior. (Response)

(7)   David killed the giant with a slingshot; he was waiting for the Savior. (Response)

(8)   Jonah was trapped in a whale; he was waiting for the Savior. (Response)

(9)   St. Joseph worked with hammer and saw while waiting for the Savior. (Response)

(10) Mary was as beautiful to God as a flower; she was waiting for the Savior. (Response)

(11) Our world today needs its Savior. (Response)

Communion Hymn: "O Little Town of Bethlehem"

Recessional: "Jesse Tree Song"

35. GIFT GIVING

Background: Certain days of the year bring out the theme of giving gifts better than others: Christmas, birthday, Easter, etc. We created this particular liturgy during Advent as a prelude to Christmas.

Opening Hymn: Organ music

Reading I: John 16:20-24 ("Ask and you will receive.")

Reading II: Luke 6:27-38 ("Give to everyone who asks you . . . you will have a great reward.")

Homily Hints: Isn't it easy to receive a gift like a new coat or a new bike? Material gifts are one thing. We are also able to give people gifts on the inside: when we tell someone we like their clothes or that they have pretty hair, or when we give them credit for doing something well.

    Now, let's give our gifts to Jesus and wait as he returns them transformed.

Offertory Hymn: "All Good Gifts"

Recessional: "Sing Praise to the Lord"

36. CHRISTMAS PAGEANT

Background: We used this liturgy to highlight the dramatic details of St. Luke's Gospel. We used a puppet skit for the homily to illustrate the Christmas theme.

Introduction: Did you celebrate your birthday last year? Can you remember back to your very first birthday? Jesus too had a birthday, and that's what we're celebrating today.

Opening Hymn: "O Come, All Ye Faithful"

Penitential Rite:
    Lector: For thinking of ourselves and not of Jesus on his birthday,
    All: Lord, we are sorry.
    Lector: For thinking of what we can get and not what we can give,
    All: Lord, we are sorry.
    Lector: For not sharing our gifts,
    All: Lord, we are sorry.

Reading I: Story and skit with puppets — using *The Story of Christmas* by Gerald Pottebaum (Pflaum, Dayton) or

your own script.

Children used puppets to illustrate the story as it was read. The children gathered behind our large altar, and their puppets could be seen by all. Their puppets were: star of Bethlehem, sad townspeople, Mary and Joseph, shepherds, angel, three kings, a manger.

Reading II: Luke 2:1-14

Homily Hints: Have a circle of children and have only one couple not hold hands in the circle. Christmas means we join hands with one another.

Right now, our singing and praying together is our way of "holding hands."

Prayers of the Faithful:
Lector: That we may treat everyone around us with love and respect, let us pray to the Lord.
All: Lord, hear our prayer.
Lector: That Jesus, who became a child like us, will help us to see the goodness in every person, let us pray to the Lord.
All: Lord, hear our prayer.

Offertory Hymn: "O Come, Little Children"

Communion Hymn: "The First Noel"

Recessional: "Joy to the World"

37. JONAH AND REPENTANCE

Background: The Lenten theme of renewal and repentance is, at the least, difficult and, at the most, impossible to get across to elementary students. This liturgy helps to bridge that gap by emphasizing the call and mission of the prophet Jonah.

We used this liturgy at a parish mass during Lent and acted out the whole story of Jonah from behind our altar by using puppets — decorated brown paper sacks tied to broom handles.

Processional: Children march in with priest and place their puppets in a cardboard box in front of the altar.

Opening Hymn: "Jonah" (A sea chanty — use first four verses for entrance and remaining verses for recessional.)

Penitential Rite:
> Celebrant: Sometimes we forget what Jesus told us. Let us think of the times we didn't show love for others and ask Jesus to help us change.
> All: Happy are those who are willing to change.
> Celebrant: For the times we did not want to forgive our friends.
> All: Happy are those who make the change.
> Celebrant: For the times we tried to hide from our mistakes.
> All: Happy are those who make the change.
> Celebrant: Help us see the ways we can share with our brothers. (Sign of Peace follows.)

Reading I: Matthew 3:1-3 (Invitation of John the Baptist, "This was his message: Repent, for the Kingdom of Heaven is at hand.")

Reading II: Book of Jonah (Cf. *The Man Caught by a Fish,* by M.M. Bremm, Arch Books, Concordia Publishing, 1967.) An adult read the story, and the children used their puppets to act out what was being said. The previous week the children had made the puppets in religion class and practiced their actions. We had these characters: Jonah, people of Nineveh, whale, one live tree and one dead tree, and a ship. We introduced each of the characters and figures for the benefit of the congregation. Then the children huddled behind the altar and used it as their stage.

Homily Hints: Two things impress me about the Book of Jonah: Jonah's unwillingness to accept his mission, and the people's conversion once Jonah decided to do his job. To bring out this theme, I used a pair of "clackers," a common toy for kids. I swung the two clackers together in the same direction — a sign of walking with God and doing what he wants. Then I swung the clackers in the opposite direction so that they would smash together — a sign of trying to run away from God.

The Mass reminds us to walk with God every day of our lives.

Prayers of the Faithful:

Lector: For the boys and girls who are trying to make good changes in their lives, let us pray to the Lord.

All: We ask this in faith.

Lector: For the people working so hard to make the changes in our church, let us pray to the Lord.

All: We ask this in faith.

Lector: For the beautiful change in the earth from winter to spring, let us pray to the Lord.

All: We ask this in faith.

Lector: For all the grown-up people who are using this Lenten

67

season to bring good changes in their lives, let us pray
to the Lord.
All: We ask this in faith.

Communion Hymn: "Hear, O Lord"

Recessional: "Jonah" (as at the beginning)

38. SACRIFICE AND SHARING

Background: The children on the intermediate level composed
this liturgy around the theme of sharing or sacrifice. To back up
their good intentions, the children returned deposit pop bottles
and used the proceeds to buy candy for the primary school
children. The theme of sharing became concrete in this action.

Opening Hymn: "Clap Your Hands"

Reading I: Acts 4:33-37 (The sacrifice of Barnabas who sold his
land and presented the money to the apostles.)

Reading II: Mark 14:32-39 (The Agony in the Garden)

Homily Hints: We can influence people's lives even when they
live far away (a letter to a friend who has moved) or
when time separates us (prayer for a dead relative).
By our sacrifice—just like Jesus did in the
garden— we can influence other lives.
In the Mass, Jesus takes away the distance
between us and the separation of time. He is here!

Offertory Hymn: "You Fill the Day"

Recessional: "The Living God"

(After Mass, we passed out the candy to the younger children.)

39. TURN TO THE LORD

Background: I asked the children what Lent meant to them, and
tried to guide the discussion along the lines of turning back to the

68

Lord, of conversion, of the traditional "metanoia" (only in words the children could understand.)

Opening Hymn: "They'll Know We Are Christians"

Penitential Rite:

> Lector: Sometimes I play rough in school and in games—and so I say,
> All: I'm sorry, Lord.
> Lector: Often I don't obey my teachers and my parents, so I say,
> All: I'm sorry, Lord.
> Lector: For the times I have run away from the things I should have done, I say,
> All: I'm sorry, Lord.

Reading I: Matthew 5:43-46 ("But I say to you: Love your enemies and pray for those who persecute you . . . for he causes his sun to rise for bad men as well as good.")

Responsorial: "Sunshine in My Soul"

Reading II: Book of Jonah (From *Children's Stories of the Bible from the Old and New Testaments,* edited by Barbara Taylor Bradford, G R Book Company, Playmore, Inc., 1968.)

Homily Hints: For this homily I played the familiar game of "Simon Says" with five students and came up with a winner. Then I compared the game to the "Lord Sez" episode with Jonah and how Jonah didn't follow God's instructions. When Jonah finally began to cooperate, we saw the results: the people turned back to the Lord.

Today we have an opportunity to turn to the Lord and offer ourselves to him. We won't run away; we'll stay, Lord.

Offertory Hymn: "Simple Gifts"

Recessional: "Joy, Joy, Joy"

40. OUR JOURNEY

Background: We used the theme of a trip as a means to emphasize Lent — a spiritual journey. This particular liturgy we celebrated at a parish Mass.

Opening Hymn: "I Have Decided to Follow Jesus"

Introduction to the Mass:
> All:Jesus, be with us always.
> Be with us good times and bad.
> Be with us this Lent.
> Travel with us.
> Lead us through the desert
> To your Easter land.

Penitential Rite:
> Celebrant: We are sorry for teasing our sisters and brothers.
> All: The Lord is good and glad to teach the proper path to all who go astray.
> Celebrant: We are sorry for fighting with others.
> All: The Lord is good and glad to teach the proper path to all who go astray.
> Celebrant: We are sorry for yelling and being grumpy with our family and friends.
> All: The Lord is good and glad to teach the proper path to all who go astray.
> Celebrant: We are sorry for doing things without permission.
> All: The Lord is good and glad to teach the proper path to all who go astray.
> Celebrant: Yahweh says this: "They had left in tears. I will comfort them as I lead them back. I will guide them to streams of water, by a smooth path where they will not stumble. For I am a father to my people."

Reading I: Psalm 119:17-20 ("Open my eyes . . . I am a wayfarer of earth.")

Responsorial:
> All: I am glad to be invited here today. Now we are standing inside the crowded city. We have come to worship and

70

praise the Lord. Pray for the peace of the world, this we ask for ourselves and all our friends.

Reading II: Deuteronomy 26:2-3 (adapted) (You must give of your harvest.)

Gospel Verse:
Lector: I am but a pilgrim here on earth.
All: I am but a pilgrim here on earth.
Lector: How I need a map; and your commands are my chart and guide.
All: I am but a pilgrim here on earth.

Reading III: Matthew 4:23-25 (Jesus preached and healed all, and they followed him.)

Homily Hints: On a journey we take a suitcase. I brought in a suitcase and asked the kids to give me examples of clothes they would bring with them. We pretended our journey is from our city to the nearest large city. The children gave me examples of what to put into the suitcase. Then we talked about how to get there. A *detour* then is going out of the way.

In our Christian lives, a detour is sin. A boy/girl detours when you won't let any of your brothers/sisters play with your friends, or when you pout if you don't get your way. This Lent, let's take Jesus along on our trips.

Prayers of the Faithful:
Lector: Help us to be strong enough not to lose our tempers.
All: Lord, show us the way.
Lector: Help us to use our talents in your work.
All: Lord, show us the way.
Lector: Help us remember to turn to you when we are unhappy or hurt.
All: Lord, show us the way.

Offertory Hymn: "All That I Am"

Communion Hymn: "Come Away"

Recessional: "It's a Long Road to Freedom"

41. A TIME FOR GIVING

Background: This liturgy was inspired during the Lenten season after I asked the students: "What do your parents give up for Lent?" It was easy then to ask what they were going to give up and what "giving up" means.

Opening Hymn: "We All Need One Another"

Penitential Rite:
> Lector: I am sorry that I hit my friends.
> All: Lord, give me strength.
> Lector: I am sorry for making fun of others.
> All: Lord, give me strength.
> Lector: I am sorry for fighting with my brothers and sisters.
> All: Lord, give me strength.

Reading I: Luke 6:27-31 ("Treat others as you would like them to treat you.")

Reading II: Matthew 6:1-10 ("When you give alms, your left hand must not know what your right is doing.")

Homily Hints: Children have various ideas of what sacrifice or "giving up" means during Lent. I first asked them what their parents "gave up" during Lent. Then I asked the children what they were doing and wrote their responses on a poster. The responses were of two kinds: negative (e.g., *not* eating candy, *not* fighting) and positive (I *will* help with dishes, I *will* eat the food on my plate).

Positive responses got a plus sign (+); negative responses got a minus sign (-). I pointed out plus signs were better. We discussed the positive ways we can "give up" things for Lent.

We give up our time to come to Church (-) but our participation today (+) brings us closer to Jesus.

Offertory Hymn: "Simple Gifts"

Communion "Of My Hands"

Recessional: "Praise God"

42. FRIENDSHIP

Background: Instead of the traditional services during Lent, our parish had a Mass on Lenten Wednesdays specially geared toward various groups: old and infirm, interfaith marriages, etc. This Mass was for youth and emphasized the theme of friendship. To bring out the theme, we passed out freshly cut spring daffodils to all who came.

Opening Hymn: "Prayer for Peace"

Penitential Rite:

Lector: For the times we have been too afraid or too busy to reach out and touch someone else,
All: Lord, forgive us.
Lector: For the times we tried to control our friends rather than help them grow,
All: Lord, forgive us.
Lector: For the times we turned away from the warmth and friendship of others,
All: Lord, forgive us.
Lector: For the times we didn't stop to help a person in need,
All: Lord, forgive us.
Lector: Lord, for the times we shut you out of our lives and did not allow you to touch us and heal us,
All: Lord, forgive us.

Reading I: Philippians 4: 4-9 ("I want you to be happy, always happy in the Lord.")

Reading II: John 15: 9-17 ("What I command you is to love one another.")

Homily Hints: Often flowers represent friendship between two people. If I give you a flower, this tells you something about me: I like you.

Just as I can reveal myself to others, so also Jesus has tried and continues to try to reveal himself to us in the Bible, in Communion, and in our lives if we remain close to him.

Communion Hymn: "The Lord Is My Shepherd"

Recessional: "The Lord Be With You"

43. VINE AND BRANCHES

Background: The students were given various Gospel passages and asked to illustrate them in some way. A group of six girls acted out the parable of the vine and branches. This liturgy came from that experience and lends itself well to a Lenten theme.

Opening Hymn: "Put Your Hand in the Hand"

Apology Time: The general theme of *growing* is very appropriate for this time — just as plants need water and nourishment so they don't dry up, we also need spiritual nourishment; when we sin we are asking to dry up.

Reading I: 1 Corinthians 3:4-9 ("Neither the planter nor the waterer matters, but God who makes things grow.")

Reading II: John 15:1-10 ("I am the vine, you are the branches.")

Homily Hints: A short skit can dramatize the Vine and Branches with two speaking parts: God the Father and Jesus Christ. Children acted out the growth of branches connected with Jesus, and the lopping off of dead wood. The dead wood was then thrown on a pile of brush near the altar.

Then the leader of the homily can ask the children how in specific ways we can remain alive in Jesus or how we "dry up," and how the Mass puts us in contact with Jesus' life.

Offertory Hymn: "Spirit of God"

Communion Hymn: Meditation by listening to the recording of "John 3,16."

Recessional: "Peace, Joy and Happiness"

44. JESUS IS ALIVE

Background: This children's Mass was our Easter Sunday celebration. This liturgy emphasizes the re-introduction of the "Gloria" after its absence during Lent and the renewal of the baptismal promises in children's words.

Procession: Celebrant walks in through congregation and wears a colorful stole.

Opening Hymn: "Praise God"

Glory to God: During Lent we eliminated the Gloria from the Mass. Now at Easter, we are joyful as if a good friend has just moved back to town. To emphasize this joy in the Gloria, we had a children's procession in which one child brought forward to the altar a large cross, decorated with flowers and wreaths and words like "life, joy, peace." The other children of the procession accompanied the cross with music — tamborines, bells and cymbals — and fresh spring flowers to decorate the altar and with baskets of Easter eggs. The children decorated the altar and prepared it for the celebration. Then we joyfully said together: Glory to God above all other things (Cf. appendix)

Reading I: John 12:24-26 ("Anyone who loves his life loses it.")

Responsorial: (Adapted from *Children's Liturgies,* by Virginia Sloyan and Gabriel Huck, The Liturgical Conference.)

Lector: No need to be afraid. He is risen. Go and tell my brothers.
All: Go and tell.
Lector: No need for alarm. He has risen. Go and tell his disciples.
All: He is risen.
Lector: Stay with us. The Lord has risen! Simon saw him!
All: Stay with us.

Lector: Why these doubts? See for yourselves. Tell all the
nations.
All: All the nations.
Lector: Peace be with you. Receive the Holy Spirit. Peace.
All: Peace

Alleluia Verse:

Cantor: Alleluia
All: Alleluia
Cantor: Jesus died so that we could live,
Let us feast with joy in the Lord.
All: Alleluia

Reading II: John 20:1-9 (Mary Magdalene at the tomb)

Homily Hints: I used two flowers, one alive, one dead. Combining
the flowers with this motto, "he who's not busy
being born, is busy dying," I tried to apply to our
lives how we share in the death and resurrection of
Christ. In our lives we see our parents fighting; our
bikes are stolen; a relative dies. Because of Jesus'
resurrection, we too can go beyond these trials and
difficulties.
Resurrection is now, and the Mass puts us in
touch with this resurrected Jesus.

Renewal of Baptismal Promises: (rewritten for children)

Celebrant: Dear children,
Lent is over and Easter is here.
To show that we want to renew our lives
on this day when Jesus renewed his life,
let us promise again what we promised when we
were baptized.
Celebrant: Do you say no to sin and selfishness?
All: I do.
Celebrant: Do you say no to ugly words and to fighting?
All: I do.
Celebrant: Do you say no to the devil who wants you to be
bad?
All: I do.

76

Celebrant: Do you believe in God the Father who made heaven and earth?

All: I do.

Celebrant: Do you believe in Jesus our Savior who died for us, who rose from the dead and is now in heaven with God the Father?

All: I do.

Celebrant: Do you believe that God will forgive your sins and that you can live forever with him in heaven?

All: I do.

Celebrant: God, the father of Jesus, has given us a new life by the water of baptism and by the Holy Spirit. May he help us to love Jesus always.

All: Amen.

Offertory Hymn: "Allelu"

Prayer Over Gifts:
We are gathered together, Father, around this table of death and life, of bread and wine.
We look at fire and see the new life of Jesus.
Only you can bring life out of death.
We offer you this bread and wine,
this life and this death,
as our offering, our sign of resurrection.
Receive our gifts.
Give us the gift of the Spirit to complete what started with bread and wine, with one life and one death.
Jesus lives when we offer this to you in his name.
Amen.

Eucharistic Acclamation: "Christ Has Died, Allelula"

Communion Hymn: "Gonna Sing My Lord"

Prayer after Communion:
It is not always Easter.
Every day is not the third day.
We go now, Father, from this rejoicing to the ordinary living of our ordinary times.
Help us to take this resurrection with us wherever we go, whatever we do.

Keep us alive and ready,
ready to give life to others.
Help us every day.
In the name of Jesus, dead and alive,
yours and ours,
today and all days,
forever and ever. Amen.

Recessional: "Praise God"

> During the recessional, the celebrant and four children pass out Easter eggs to children and adults present as a joyful remembrance of the "Jesus is alive" liturgy.

45. CELEBRATE LIFE

Background: This liturgy emphasizes the theme of life — a theme we thought applicable to parish liturgies after Easter. We used this theme at a children's Sunday liturgy and tied it in with the new life Jesus won for us through his death *and* resurrection.

Opening Hymn: "Alive in Christ"

Introduction to the Mass: We have here a real Christian family — parents, children, other adults — and we all have in common our one savior and brother, Jesus Christ.

Penitential Rite:
Celebrant: Sometimes, when we forget that God truly lives in us, we become cranky or angry. For those times,
All: We are sorry, Lord.
Celebrant: Other times, when we don't remember that God lives in others, we hurt them with our words or even our hands. For those times,
All: We are sorry, Lord.
Celebrant: For the times when we do not show love and respect for all life — people, animals, plants,
All: We are sorry, Lord.

78

Celebrant: Thank you, Lord Jesus, for making us able to love others and to love you. We are alive with your gifts. We say with joy, Lord, how wonderful you are to each of us.

Reading I: John 12:24-26 (adapted) (Jesus compares us to a wheat grain that dies but grows into a new plant and rich harvest.)

Responsorial:

Lector: Our brother Jesus rose from the dead.
All: Our brother Jesus rose from the dead.
Lector: He reminds us that we have resurrection every day.
All: Our brother Jesus rose from the dead.

Lector: When we hope,
All: Our brother Jesus rose from the dead.
Lector: When we help,
All: Our brother Jesus rose from the dead.
Lector: When we forgive,
All: Our brother Jesus rose from the dead.
Lector: When we trust,
All: Our brother Jesus rose from the dead.
Lector: We come to life again,
All: Jesus lives in us!

Alleluia Verse: "Alleluia! We Will Hear Your Word"

Reading II: John 5:19-20, 26 (adapted) (The Father gives new life through Jesus, "For the Father, who is the source of life, has made the Son the source of life.")

Homily Hints: I took three objects: a potted, blooming flower; a plastic flower; a cut flower. I asked, "Boys and girls, what's the difference between these three flowers?" "One has roots," a child responded.

From this answer, I expanded on the theme that we all need to be rooted in something, in someone. Jesus becomes our soil, our strength. Then I made applications to various groups of people — kids, adults, college students, etc.

The Easter event is God's way of telling us that Jesus has life, that he has blossomed. Each Eucharist is a flowering of Easter.

Prayers of the Faithful:
Lector: That we, like a living flower, may be rooted in Jesus, our savior and brother,
All: Lord, hear our prayer.
Lector: That we may let our sins and selfishness die so that we can share the new life of Jesus,
All: Lord, hear our prayer.
Lector: That our souls will open to God's love like the flowers open to the sun,
All: Lord, hear our prayer.
Lector: That we may share the new life of Jesus with everyone we know, especially our families,
All: Lord, hear our prayer.

Offertory Hymn: "Take Our Bread"

Communion Hymn: "La, La, Life"

Recessional: "Thank You, Lord"

46. FORGIVENESS

Background: For this parish liturgy we had two banners, a "smiley" and a "frownie," with these captions:

Opening Hymn: "Peace Time"

Introduction: Jesus said, "If your brother sins against you seven times a day, and seven times a day turns back to you saying, 'I'm sorry,' forgive him." As the Easter season begins, we want to change ourselves so that we can be more forgiving to people who hurt us. And we want to learn to say, "I'm sorry," and to ask forgiveness when we have hurt others.

Penitential Rite:

Celebrant: Do I forgive those who hurt my feelings? (Pause after each question.)

Do I forgive my parents when I think they are wrong?

Do I forgive those who don't like me?

Do I forgive others even when I feel they are at fault?

Do I forgive my brothers and sisters when they get into my things?

Do I forgive those who won't share with me?

Lord, forgive us for the times we have hurt you in our neighbor. Help us to understand that if we don't find you here in the people we meet, we won't find you in heaven. Give us the strength to forgive even our enemies so that your love may replace our hatred.

Reading I: Matthew 5: 43-45 (adapted) (Love and pray for all.) Jesus said, "There is a saying, 'Love your friends and hate your enemies.' But *I* say: Love your enemies. Pray

81

for those who hurt you! Remember, God sends sunlight and rain to both bad and good people. If you love only those who love you, you are no better than anyone else. There's nothing great about loaning money to someone who will pay you back; you must give when you don't expect to be paid back. You must be like God, who loves everyone."

Responsorial: Psalm 32:1-5 (adapted) (Confess and he will forgive.)

Lector: Ask the Lord, and he will forgive.
All: Ask the Lord, and he will forgive.
Lector: Happy are those people whose sin is forgiven.
All: Ask the Lord, and he will forgive.
Lector: At first I was afraid to confess my sins, but nothing I did made me happy.
All: Ask the Lord, and he will forgive.
Lector: When I came to you, Lord, my sins evaporated like water on a sunny day.
All: Ask the Lord, and he will forgive.

Reading II: Matthew 5:23-25 (adapted) (Settle differences now.) Jesus said: "If you are in church, praying to God, and you remember that you and your friend have had a fight, go first and make up with your friend, and then come to church. Then God will listen to your prayers."

Alleluia Verse:.
Lector: Alleluia
All: Alleluia
Lector: Forgive us for the times we have done wrong, as we forgive those who have hurt us.
All: Alleluia

Reading III: Matthew 18:23-35 (Parable of the unforgiving servant) Or Luke 5:27-38 (Help sinners; Jesus forgave them, "I have not come to call the virtuous, but sinners to repentance.")

Homily Hints: (Place the Easter candle in the middle aisle.) Flu and colds were going around at the time of this homily. I first asked how many had colds; then I talked of two kinds of healing. The physical healing of our bodies and the spiritual healing of our hearts. Jesus, as seen in the Easter candle, can heal our hearts. (Then light the Easter candle.)

I then demonstrated the two banners — smiley and frownie — and told everyone that I was going to use three examples of "frownies" and how they could be turned into "smileys" through the healing that Jesus gives.

Example 1: An older brother picks on a younger one who had called the older one "names." Show the frownie.
Healing: While placing my hands on the Easter candle, I portrayed each of the brothers asking for forgiveness. Show smiley.

Example 2: A little girl wants to stay up and watch a good TV program even though she has school tomorrow and has a bad cold. She is nasty when her mother says no. Show frownie.
Healing: I portrayed the little girl asking forgiveness for being nasty when her mother said no for her benefit. Show smiley.

Example 3: Both parents go to an evening party. The next day, having had too much to drink the night before, they scold the children undeservedly. Show the frownie.
Healing: I explained that the next day they apologized to the children and tell them that parents make mistakes too. Show smiley.

Conclusion: At Mass, Jesus wants us to be a "smiley," not a "frownie," and carry our smile out the door with us.

Prayers of the Faithful:
Lector: That we may forgive those who hurt us,
All: Lord, hear our prayer.

Lector: That we may forgive teachers when we feel we are
        right and they are wrong,
All: Lord, hear our prayer.
Lector: That nations will learn to forgive each other so that war
        will end,
All: Lord, hear our prayer.
Lector: That we will be willing to say, "I'm sorry," when we
        have hurt others,
All: Lord, hear our prayer.
Lector: That we will try harder to forgive our parents when we
        think they have been unfair,
All: Lord, hear our prayer.
Lector: That our parents will be willing to forgive and forget
        when we are really trying to do better,
All: Lord, hear our prayer.

Offertory Hymn: "Love One Another"

Communion Hymn: "They'll Know We Are Christians"

Recessional: "Peace Time"

47. CHRIST, THE LIGHT OF THE WORLD

Background: The experiences of light and dark speak to children. Often they are afraid of the dark and can identify with the light of even one little candle. For this liturgy, we placed the Easter candle in front of the altar and used its light for the Liturgy of the Word; only during the Liturgy of the Eucharist did we turn on the electric lights.

Opening Hymn: "The King of Glory"

Reading I: 1 John 1:5-7 (Live in the light of God, "a light the darkness could not overpower.")

Responsorial: Psalm 27 ("Yahweh is my light and my salvation.")

Reading II: John 12:46-50 ("I, the light have come into the world, so that whoever believes in me need not stay in the dark any more.")

Homily Hints: An effective means of getting across to children the value that Christ is with us is to use birthday candles — especially the kind that lose their flame when you blow on them but then flame up again 10 seconds later. I've used these candles to show how Christ as our light is still with us even when all looks dark.

His word gives hope to our experience. His sacrifice gives hope to our trials and difficulties.

Offertory Hymn: "Of My Hands"

Communion Hymn: "Spirit of God"

Recessional: "Prayer of St. Francis"

48. ASCENSION

Background: We used this liturgy to bring out to the children the fact that Jesus is going home to the Father. Helium balloons of various colors (designated "the apostles") were helpful, especially if one is designated "Jesus" and another "Spirit." Then the leader or priest can carry the "Jesus" balloon out and the "Spirit" balloon can join the "apostles" balloons.

Opening Hymn: "Here We Are"

Greeting:
Celebrant: Let us worship the Lord for he is our God.
All: And we are his children.

Penitential Rite:
Celebrant: Sometimes we forget what Jesus told us and we don't act as if we love each other. Let us think of the times we didn't show love for others and ask for pardon. For the times we said we would run away from home,
All: We are sorry.
Celebrant: For the times we would not share with others,
All: We are sorry.
Celebrant: For the times we disobeyed our parents and teachers,

85

All: We are sorry.

Celebrant: For the times we did not help someone who needed us,

All: We are sorry.

Celebrant: For the times we took things that belonged to others,

All: We are sorry.

Celebrant: For the times we didn't tell the truth,

All: We are sorry.

Celebrant: To show that we do love our brothers and sisters, let us offer each other the sign of peace.

Opening Prayer:

Celebrant: Our Father in heaven, this is the day we think of your Son coming home to you, and we are glad that we can go home to our families, too.

Reading I: Acts 1:3, 7-11 (Jesus announces the eventual coming of the Spirit, and ascends into heaven.)

Responsorial: Psalm 23:6

All: Your goodness and love will be with me as long as I live, and your house will be my home forever.

Reading II: Matthew 28:16-20 (Jesus' command to preach and baptize and his promise of remaining with us always.)

Homily Hints: (1) Re-enact with colored balloons the going-away of Jesus and the coming of the Spirit.
(2) Use an uninflated balloon to signify that the Apostles were lost and really flat without him.
Blow up the balloon and have it signify the gift of the Spirit Jesus sent when he went home to the Father.
Each Ascension Thursday Mass helps us remember that we still have the Spirit among us.

Offertory Hymn: "Take Our Bread"

Prayer Over The Gifts:

Celebrant: Accept the prayers and offerings of your children, O Lord, and let our love for you help us remember that we, too, can go home to you someday.

86

Communion Hymn: "They'll Know We Are Christians" (This song tells of the positive responses the Spirit inspires in us.)

Recessional: "Here We Are"

49. FEAST OF ST. FRANCIS
HARMONY IN CREATION

Background: The changing of seasons near the feast of St. Francis of Assisi (October 4) always presents a unique opportunity to consider the theme of creation. In this liturgy, I wanted to expose the kids to St. Francis and his way of seeing harmony in all of creation.

Opening Hymn: "Everything Is Beautiful"

Reading I: St. Francis' "The Canticle of Brother Sun" (from *The Writings of St. Francis of Assisi,* translated by Benen Fahey, O.F.M. Copyright ©1964, Franciscan Herald Press.

Most high, all-powerful, all good, Lord!
   All praise is yours, all glory, all honor
   And all blessing.
To you, alone, Most High, do they belong.
   No mortal lips are worthy
   To pronounce your name.
All praise be yours, my Lord, through all that you have made,
   And first my lord Brother Sun,
   Who brings the day; and light you give to us through him.
How beautiful is he, how radiant in all his splendor!
   Of you, Most High, he bears the likeness.
All praise be yours, my Lord, through Sisters Moon and Stars;
   In the heavens you have made them, bright
   And precious and fair.
All praise be yours, my Lord, through Brothers Wind and Air;
   And fair and stormy, all the weather's moods,
   By which you cherish all that you have made.
All praise be yours, my Lord, through Sister Water,

So useful, lowly, precious and pure.
All praise be yours, my Lord, through Brother Fire,
   Through whom you brighten up the night.
   How beautiful is he, how gay! Full of power and strength.
All praise be yours, my Lord, through Sister Earth, our mother
   Who feeds us in her sovereignty and produces
   Various fruits with colored flowers and herbs.
All praise be yours, my Lord, through those who grant pardon
   For love of you; through those who endure
   Sickness and trial.
Happy those who endure in peace,
   By you, Most High, they will be crowned.
All praise be yours, my Lord, through Sister Death,
   From whose embrace no mortal can escape.
Woe to those who die in mortal sin!
   Happy those She finds doing your will!
   The second death can do no harm to them.
Praise and bless my Lord, and give him thanks,
   And serve him with great humility.

Responsorial: Psalm 118 (Adapted into choir form)

Lector: Oh, give thanks to the Lord, for he is good,
All: His loving kindness continues forever.
Lector: Give thanks to the God of gods,
All: For his loving kindness continues forever.
Lector: Give thanks to the Lord of lords,
All: For his loving kindness continues forever.
Lector: Praise him who alone does mighty miracles,
All: For his loving kindness continues forever.
Lector: Praise him who planted the water within the earth,
All: For his loving kindness continues forever.
Lector: Praise him who made the heavenly lights,
All: For his loving kindness continues forever.
Lector: The sun to rule the day,
All: For his loving kindness continues forever.
Lector: And the moon and stars at night,
All: For his loving kindness continues forever.
Lector: He gives food to every living thing,
All: For his loving kindness continues forever.

Reading II: Luke 10:1-13 (Jesus sends out his disciples in pairs, "Whatever house you go into let your first words be, 'Peace to this house.'")

Homily Hints: There's a story about St. Francis making himself a friend with the so-called ferocious wolf of Gubbio. (Cf. Murray Bodo's *Francis: The Journey and the Dream,* St. Anthony Messenger Press, 1972, pp. 71-75.) Francis found peace with the wolf in these words (p. 75):

"Francis spoke again. 'Brother Wolf, in the name of Jesus, our brother, I have come for you. We need you in the city. These people here have come with me to ask you, great ferocious one, to be the guardian and protector of Gubbio. In return we offer you respect and shelter for as long as you live. In pledge of this I offer you my hand.'

"He stretched out his hand. The wolf seemed calm, but he remained immobile, scanning the crowd with his large, bloodshot eyes. Then slowly he walked to Francis and lifted his paw into his warm, steady hand. The two remained in that position for a long time and what they said to one another Francis never told to any living soul.

"Finally, Francis leaned over and put his arms about the wolf's neck. Then he and his new brother walked meekly up to the brave peasant woman and the three of them led the stunned, silent crowd back to Gubbio."

Sometimes we're afraid too — of the dark, of meeting new people, of being all alone. Jesus helps us feel at-one-ment (harmony) with people and all of nature. With him near us, we are never alone.

He is here today at our Mass — let us invite him to be with us.

Offertory Hymn: "Prayer of St. Francis"

Communion Hymn: "Thank You"

Recessional: "You Fill the Day"

89

50. HALLOWEEN

Background: We have used this liturgy for the general parish Mass on the eve of All Saints. The response has been enthusiastic. We invite all children to come dressed up in their costumes, and then we bring out what those costumes mean at the homily. (Adapted from *Religion Teacher's Journal,* October, 1971.)

Opening Hymn: "Halloween Song" (The entrance procession can include the celebrant and a number of children in costume.) Here at Sacred Heart our church is *full* for this liturgy, half children, half adults.

Penitential Rite:
Celebrant: Sometimes we forget what Jesus told us and we don't act like we love each other. Let us think of the times we didn't show love for others and ask for forgiveness. For the times we said we would run away from home,
All: We are sorry,
Celebrant: For the times we wouldn't let people play with us,
All: We are sorry.
Celebrant: For the times we didn't listen to our parents and teachers,
All: We are sorry.
Celebrant: For the times we turned our backs on people who needed us,
All: We are sorry.
Celebrant: For the times we put a mask on to hide from other people,
All: We are sorry.

Opening Prayer: God our Father, help us to celebrate this happy day. As we put on costumes to play and have fun as brothers and sisters of Jesus, let us remember to love one another as he did.

Reading I: Psalm 150 (Praise God.)

Responsorial: Our God is a God who loves all people.
People small, people tall,

People with long hair or no hair at all.
People old, people new,
People just like me and you.
People who dance, people who sing,
People who might do anything.
I will love all people as our God does.
Happy the people who share God's love.

Reading II: Acts 9: 1-6, 20-22, 27-29 (Paul's conversion)

Reading III: Mark 10: 13 (Jesus welcomes the children.)

Homily Hints: Show the children a mirror and ask them about the faces they see there. Some faces will be ghoulish animals, some witches, some hobos, etc. Often our faces are happy or sad: we win a game, we pout in corners, we resent the babysitter coming again.

The secret of Halloween is that Jesus loves us as we are, so we don't need to wear masks. Take your mask off, just as St. Paul took his mask off. Take off your *masks,* now!

Offertory Hymn: "Take Our Bread"
(This time of year we found it meaningful to collect comic books, coloring books, toys, etc., for the pediatric wards of our city hospitals.)

Prayer over the Gifts: Accept the prayers and offerings of your children, O Lord, and let our love for you help us to love each other. We ask this through Christ, our Lord.

Communion Hymn: "Sons of God"

Recessional: "When the Saints Go Marching In"

51. THE THINGS WE ARE THANKFUL FOR

Background: We used this liturgy at a regular parish Mass. The children participated by helping to read, by taking the dialogue parts in the Gospel, by leading the singing, and by forming the processions. The theme of "thankfulness" is often appropriate, especially around Thanksgiving Day.

Opening Hymn: "Sing Praise to the Lord"

Penitential Rite:
>   Celebrant: We are sorry for the times when we didn't have patience enough to listen to the other side of an argument.
>   All: Happy are those who listen.
>   Celebrant: We are sorry for not appreciating an older brother or sister until he or she left home.
>   All: Happy are those who appreciate people.
>   Celebrant: We are sorry for the times when we have taken for granted relatives or friends until they have died or moved away.
>   All: Happy are we when we are thankful for people who live with us.

Reading I: Psalm 100 (An invitation to praise God)

Reading II: Matthew 7:11-12 ("Give us today our daily bread!")

Reading III: Luke 17:11-19 (The 10 Lepers)
>   I divided the Gospel up into four speaking parts: a leader, 10 lepers, Jesus, and the healed leper. We memorized the lines and then acted them out on the steps of the sanctuary. This procedure involved many

92

of the children and expressed visibly the theme of thankfulness.

Leader: As Jesus and his apostles continued onward toward Jerusalem, they reached the border between the countries of Galilee and Samaria, a foreign country. As they entered a village there, 10 lepers stood at a distance shouting:

10 Lepers: Jesus, have mercy on us.

Leader: Jesus looked at them and said:

Jesus: Go to the Jewish priest and show him that you are healed.

Leader: And as they were going, their leprosy disappeared. One of them came back to Jesus, shouting:

One Leper: Glory to God, I'm healed.

Leader: He fell flat on the ground in front of Jesus, face downward, thanking Jesus for what he had done. This man was a foreigner, a Samaritan. Jesus asked:

Jesus: Did I not heal 10 men? Where are the other nine? Does only this foreigner return to give glory to God?

Leader: And Jesus said to the man who returned to give him thanks:

Jesus: Stand up and go; your faith has made you well.

At Mass we continue to thank Jesus for what he has given us.

Prayers of the Faithful:
Respond with: "Thanks be to God."

Offertory Hymn: "Take Our Bread"

Communion Hymn: "Thanks for the Chance"

Recessional: "He's Got the Whole World in His Hands"

IV First Communion Penance

52. FIRST COMMUNION (1)

(Lou and Glenn Heese family
and especially Anne)

Background: Many children in our parish make their first communion through the occasion of a home Mass. A home Mass gives the priest, child and parents an opportunity to plan the special occasion.

Introduction: Word of welcome by one of the parents. (The child to receive first communion has invited over friends, playmates, teachers, etc.)

Opening Hymn: "Allelu"

Penitential Rite:
>Child: For sometimes forgetting to be kind and loving to my family and friends,
>All: I am sorry, Lord.
>Child: For sometimes forgetting to say, "Good morning, Jesus."
>All: I am sorry, Lord.
>Child: For not having Jesus in my heart,
>All: I am sorry, Lord. .

Reading I and Responsorial: "Children" (by Johnny Cash, *Gospel Road* album)

Reading II: 1 Corinthians 12:31-13:12 (Love is the highest of spiritual gifts; the knowledge I have now is imperfect.) The reading applies in that it helps us see first communion as an initial step; later, it will be understood by the child in greater depth.

Reading III: John 15:5-8 ("I am the vine, you are the branches.")

Prayers of the Faithful:
>Lector: That people may love God more and remember they are his children, let us pray to the Lord.
>All: Lord, hear our prayer.
>Lector: That our families and friends stay well, let us pray to the Lord.
>All: Lord, hear our prayer.
>Lector: That Jews and Arabs stop fighting, let us pray to the Lord.
>All: Lord, hear our prayer.
>Lector: That Anne (first communicant) may grow closer to Jesus everyday, let us pray to the Lord.
>All: Lord, hear our prayer.

Offertory Hymn: "Take Our Bread"

Communion Meditation (by a parent): Let us all join hands to show we are truly Christ's community in union with him and with each other. May our love for one another grow and blossom and the seeds of our love scatter to where

only God knows the good they reap.
    May the Holy Spirit, at home within us,
continue to reveal Jesus to Anne and to
us all.

Recessional: "Sunshine in My Soul"

53. FIRST COMMUNION (2)

(Phil and Rita Wurtz family,
especially Mary Aileene)

Background: An eight-year-old girl wanted to make her first communion at home; so she, her parents and I put together this liturgy. Her aunts, uncles and grandparents came to help celebrate, and we all shared a late afternoon meal to end the day. (Guitar music was provided by an aunt and uncle.)

Opening Hymn: "This Is the Day"

Penitential Rite: A fine opportunity in the home setting to reconcile fights, quarrels and arguments.

Reading I: 1 Corinthians 12:14-21;26-27 ("Now you together are Christ's body, but each of you is a different part of it.")

Reading II: John 20:19-31 (Thomas comes to believe that Christ rose from the dead.)

97

Homily Hints: Think of putting together a picture puzzle. Then, imagine each of us as a piece in the puzzle of life. We are all united and need each other to portray the entire picture. Even the young person about to receive communion for the first time is important to the Church. Let's let her enthusiasm in receiving her first communion recharge our desire to be near Christ.

Prayers of the Faithful: (After each petition, sing the refrain of "Hear O Lord.")

Sign of Peace: "Let There Be Peace on Earth"

Recessional: "Go in Peace"

54. FIRST CONFESSION SERVICE

Background: This service is an expanded first confession ceremony for intermediate students. It puts the sacrament of Penance within an awareness of social sin and forgiveness. When we used this ceremony, some children who had already received the sacrament were present along with those who were receiving it for the first time. Although we used the service by itself, it could be celebrated in conjunction with the Eucharist.

This service was adapted from material prepared by the Children's Liturgy Committee, Diocese of Baton Rouge, Box 2028, Baton Rouge, LA 70821.

Opening Hymn: "Here We Are"
(Sung while the celebrant processes in with two students carrying candle and Bible.)

Introduction: Celebrant explains in his own words the significance of the sacrament of Penance, especially for those receiving it for the first time.

Opening Prayer:
All: O God, I trust you.
No one who waits for you will ever have to feel ashamed.

Lord, teach me your ways; lead me in your paths.
You, O Lord, can help me.
Because of your great mercy, Lord, forgive me.

Reading I: Luke 15:11-33 (The parable of the Prodigal Son)

Response:

All: We were dead and now we will live again.
We were sad and now we will laugh again.
We join together to praise the Lord.
Our brother Jesus will rise from the dead.
He reminds us that we have resurrection and
forgiveness everyday.
When we love and don't hate,
When we help and don't hurt,
When we try and don't give up,
When we forgive and don't hold a grudge.
Today we come to life again—
Jesus lives in us.

Homily Hints: To highlight our solidarity as one Christian family
and to point out that personal sin has social
implications, I got the children into a circle, had
them join hands, and then asked one boy to drop out
of the circle. "What happened?" I asked.
When we have five basketball players, or nine
baseball players, the team needs each player and
one affects the whole team.
From this basis, it's easy to draw out implications
of the communal confession.

Examination of Conscience:

Celebrant: Let us be like the Prodigal Son by having
confidence in God's forgiveness.
All: I will get up and go to my Father and will say to him,
"Father, I have sinned against heaven and in your eyes.
I don't deserve to be called your son or daughter
anymore."
Lord, we ask that you make us clean and have mercy on
us.
Celebrant: We already know God's two great commandments

of love. Let us say very slowly in our hearts God's first commandment of love.

All: Love God with all your heart.

Celebrant: Now, let's ask ourselves if we are keeping that commandment.

Am I really loving God, my Father?

He wants me to speak to him often. Do I pray to him from my heart? In private and in the Mass?

My name is special. Do I use God's name with love and respect?

Do I find time to thank God for my talents and gifts and abilities, or do I just want to play and not think about him?

Can I really feel God's love through the love my parents and friends give me?

Celebrant: Let us say slowly in our hearts God's second commandment.

All: Love your neighbor as yourself.

Celebrant: Let's ask ourselves if we are keeping this command of God.

Do I insist on my own way and not care about the other person's idea?

Do I make fun of people I don't like because of their clothes, or where they live, or because they don't like the same games that I do?

Do I disobey my parents by not doing the chores around the house?

Do I lie to get out of something?

(Silent examination of conscience should follow.)

Act of Contrition:

All: Lord, forgive us for the times we have hurt you in our neighbor. Help us to understand that if we don't find you here in the people we meet, we won't find you in heaven. Give us the strength to use our talents to help others to know and love you more. Grant us the courage to admit our faults and to change our ways. This we ask through Christ our Lord.

100

Individual Confessions: (While those who want to receive the sacrament of Penance participate in it, the other members of the group signify their oneness with those confessing by joining in singing songs like "Kum Ba Ya" or "Whatsoever You Do.")

Absolution and Assigning of Penance: Celebrant

Recessional: "Allelu"

55. PEACE THROUGH FORGIVENESS

Background: This service was adapted from material prepared by the Children's Liturgy Committee, Diocese of Baton Rouge, Box 2028, Baton Rouge, LA 70821.

Opening Hymn: "I Must Remember"

Reading I: John 20:19-23 ("For those whose sins you forgive, they are forgiven.")
Introduction: Ever since Christ walked this earth, man has lived in an atmosphere of mercy. God in his gracious love gave us the sacrament of Penance to be our peace. If God who is all holy is willing to forgive us our sins, shouldn't we be willing to forgive one another?

Reading II: Matthew 18:21-35 ("Lord, how often must I forgive my brother?")
Introduction: Each of us easily sees the injustice of the first servant and yet at times we are that "unjust servant." We rely on the mercy of God toward ourselves, but are not willing to forgive those who have offended us. We are quick to ask forgiveness for ourselves but slow to grant pardon to our brother.

101

Examination of Conscience:
Let us think for.a few moments of the times we have been unwilling to forgive our neighbor, realizing that only if we forgive others will we be forgiven.
Have I forgiven:
Those who hurt my feelings? (pause)
Those who don't like me?
Those who misused the things I shared with them?
Those who rashly judge me?
Those who are jealous of me?
Those who wouldn't let me share with them?

(Pause for silent reflection.)

Let us thoughtfully sing the "Our Father."

Confession of Guilt: based on Psalm 51 (Prayer of repentance and confidence in God.)

(Alternate sides.)
1. Have mercy on me, O God, in your goodness.
2. In the greatness of your compassion, wipe out all my faults.
1. Thoroughly wash me from my guilt.
2. And of my sin cleanse me.
1. Our Lord identified with the people whom Paul persecuted.
2. Lord, help us to realize that what we do to our neighbor you consider done to yourself.
1. Paul's eyes were opened and he was filled with the Holy Spirit.
2. Send your Spirit, Lord, that we may see more clearly your will for us.
1. Paul was willing to change his way of life.
2. Lord, help us to dare to change our way of life for you.

Celebrant: Let us silently think of the ways we might need to change our lives, so we may show to others the love God has for us and that we in turn give glory to God for the changes in our lives. (Pause)

Act of Contrition:
All: Lord, forgive us for the times we have hurt you in our neighbor. Help us to understand that if we don't find you

102

here in the people we meet, we won't find you in heaven. Give us the strength to use our talents to help others to know and love you more. Grant us the courage to admit our faults and to change our ways. We ask this and all things through Christ our Lord. Amen.

(Individual confessions could be heard now.)

Meditation: Listen to the recording of "Lord, Give Me a Heart of Flesh" by Joe Wise.

Recessional: "Peace, My Friends"

Appendix

I. SIMPLIFIED LITURGICAL PRAYERS

Glory to God

Glory to God above all other things.

And peace to everyone.

O mighty king, we adore you, we thank you,

We praise you because you are great.

Lord, Jesus, Lamb of God,

You take away our sins, forgive us.

You are the Father's right-hand man,

Hear our prayer.

You, Jesus, are our Holy Lord and King,

With the Holy Spirit and God the Father. Amen.

Creed

(God, the Father)   I believe that God the Father is the Creator
of all things.

(Jesus)   I believe that Jesus Christ is the Son of God.

I believe that he loves us, loves us dearly.

I believe that he lives, lives in us.

I believe that he died, died for us.

I believe that he will return, return to live
with us for all eternity.

(Holy Spirit)   I believe that God, the Holy Spirit, tells us
what to do.

I believe that his words of wisdom help us
become the true persons that God
created us to be.

Prayer over the Gifts

Celebrant: Father, here is the bread. Here is the wine.

Soon, this bread and this wine will be changed

into the body and blood of Jesus.

Father, here *we* are.

Change us, too. Make us holy.

Make us like your son, Jesus.

We ask this through the name of Jesus.

Prepared by the Children's Liturgy Committee, Diocese of Baton
Rouge, Box 2028, Baton Rouge, LA 70821.

II. SUGGESTIONS FOR MUSIC

The following is a listing (by no means exhaustive) of songs and hymns, some of which are used in the book, suitable for liturgies for children. The listing is arranged alphabetically according to title and includes the author and at least one source where the songs may be found. Following each listing is a letter which indicates for what part of a liturgy the hymn or song may be appropriate: E = entrance, O = offertory, C = communion, R = recessional, S = special (response, acclamation, meditation, etc.).

Alive in Christ Lou Fortunate	*Songs for the Eucharist* Wm. H. Sadlier	E
All Good Gifts Stephen Schwartz	*Godspell* (recording) Volando Publishing 1700 Broadway New York, NY 10019	O
All I Am, I Give to You Joe Wise	*A New Day* (recording) WLP	O
All That I Am Sebastian Temple	*Young People's Folk Hymnal* WLP	O
All the Earth Lucien Deiss	*Young People's Folk Hymnal* WLP	E
Allelu Ray Repp	*Hymnal for Young Christians* FEL	R
Allelula! We Will Hear Your Word Joe Wise	*Welcome In* (recording) NALR	S
Amazing Grace John Newton	*Folk Hymnal for the Now Generation* Zondervan	CS
Anthem Neil Diamond	*Jonathan Livingston Seagull* Alfred Publishing Company 75 Channel Drive Port Washington, NY 11050	S
Battle Hymn of the Republic Julia Ward Howe	traditional	R
Be a New Man Joe Wise	*A New Day* (recording) WLP	E
Bless the Lord Clarence Rivers	*Hymnal for Young Christians* FEL	E

107

Blowing in the Wind Bob Dylan	Warner Brothers Publishing 1230 Avenue of the Americas New York, NY 10020	E
Children's Creed Mary Braida	*God Made Us a Family* (recording) Mary Braida	C
Christ Has Died, Alleluia Joe Wise	*A New Day* (recording) WLP	S
Clap Your Hands Ray Repp	*Hymnal for Young Christians* FEL	E
Come Away Ray Repp	*Hymnal for Young Christians* FEL	CR
Come Holy Ghost Caswall-Lambilotte	*People's Mass Book* WLP	E
Come Out Jack Miffleton	*Come Out* (recording) WLP	E
Dear Father Neil Diamond	*Jonathan Livingston Seagull* Alfred Publishing Company 75 Channel Drive Port Washington, NY 11050	C
Enter, Rejoice and Come in Author unknown		E
Even a Worm Jack Miffleton	*Even a Worm* (recording) WLP	S
Everybody's Got to Grow Jack Miffleton	*Even a Worm* (recording) WLP	ES
Everything Is Beautiful Ray Stevens	Ahab Music Company 1708 Grand Avenue Nashville, TN 37212	EO
Fill It With Sunshine Joe Wise	*Close Your Eyes, I Got a Surprise* (recording) NALR	S
Fill My Cup Richard Blanchard	*Sing 'n Celebrate* Word	C
Go in Peace Sonny Salsbury	*Sing 'n Celebrate* Word	R
God Bless America Irving Berlin	Irving Berlin Music Corp. 1290 Avenue of the Americas New York, NY 10019	R
God Made Us All Jack Miffleton	*Come Out* (recording) WLP	E

Gonna Sing, My Lord Joe Wise	*Young People's Folk Hymnal* WLP	**CR**
Halloween Song Neil Blunt	*Come Out* (recording) WLP	**R**
Hear, O Lord Ray Repp	*Hymnal for Young Christians* FEL	**O**
Hello Song Neil Blunt	*Come Out* (recording) WLP	**E**
Here We Are Ray Repp	*Hymnal for Young Christians* FEL	**E**
He's Got the Whole World spiritual	*Folk Hymnal for the Now Generation* Zondervan	**R**
Hey Day! Jack Miffleton	*Even a Worm* (recording) WLP	**ER**
His Banner Over Me Is Love anonymous-Carey Landry	*Hi God* (recording) NALR	**R**
Holy God, We Praise Thy Name Ignaz Franz	*People's Mass Book* WLP	**R**
House Upon the Rocks Mary Braida	*God Made Us a Family* (recording) Mary Braida	**OS**
I Believe in You Joe Wise	*Close Your Eyes, I Got a Surprise* (recording) NALR	**S**
I Have Decided to Follow Jesus traditional	*Folk Hymnal for the Now Generation* Zondervan	**E**
I Know a Place Mary Braida	*God Made Us a Family* (recording) Mary Braida	**ES**
I Must Remember Lou Fortunate	*Songs for Penance* Wm. H. Sadlier	**E**
I Want to Learn More About You Lou Fortunate	*Songs for Jesus Our Lord* Wm. H. Sadlier	**S**
I'll Be There Joe Wise	*Welcome In* (recording) NALR	**S**
I've Got Peace Like a River spiritual	*Sing 'n Celebrate* Word	**C**
Immaculate Mary traditional Lourdes hymn	*People's Mass Book* WLP	**RS**
Isn't the Love of Jesus Something J. Peterson	*Folk Hymnal for the Now Generation* Zondervan	**E**

109

It's a Long Road to Freedom Miriam Theresa Winter	*Joy Is Like the Rain* (recording) Vanguard	**ER**
Jesse Tree Song Jack Miffleton	*Come Out* (recording) WLP	**E**
John 3,16 Mary Braida	*God Made Us a Family* (recording) Mary Braida	**CS**
Jonah E. J. Bash	*Song Book for Saints and Sinners* Agape	**E**
Joy Is Like the Rain Miriam Theresa Winter	*Joy Is Like the Rain* (recording) Vanguard	**EC**
Joy, Joy, Joy traditional	*Songs for the Eucharist* Wm. H. Sadlier	**E**
The King of Glory W. F. Jabusch	*Hymnal for Young Christians* FEL	**E**
The Kingdom of God Lou Fortunate	*Songs for Jesus Our Lord* Wm. H. Sadlier	**E**
Knock on Any Door	*Joy* Magazine, third grade edition, Spring, 1974	**E**
Kum Ba Yah African folk song	*Folk Hymnal for the Now Generation* Zondervan	**C**
La La Life Jack Miffleton	*Come Out* (recording) WLP	**C**
Let There Be Peace on Earth Sy Miller and Jill Jackson	Shawnee Press, Inc. Delaware Water Gap, PA	**E**
Let Us Break Bread Together spiritual	*Hymnal for Young Christians* FEL	**O**
Let's Build Peace Mary Braida	*God Made Us a Family* (recording) Mary Braida	**OS**
The Living God Sebastian Temple	*Young People's Folk Hymnal* WLP	**R**
The Lord Be With You Paul Quinlan	*Hymnal for Young Christians* FEL	**E**
Lord, Give Me a Heart of Flesh Joe Wise	*A New Day* (recording) WLP	**CR**
Lord Have Mercy Ray Repp	*Hymnal for Young Christians* FEL	**S**
The Lord Is My Shepherd Robert Blue	*Hymnal for Young Christians* FEL	**C**

110

Love One Another Germaine Habjan	*Hymnal for Young Christians* FEL	O
Magical Box Elaine Curzio	*Songs for Jesus Our Lord* Wm. H. Sadlier	R
The Mass Is Ended Sebastian Temple	*Young People's Folk Hymnal* WLP	R
Michael Row the Boat Ashore slave song	*Song Book for Saints and Sinners* Agape	E
My Country 'Tis of Thee Samuel Francis Smith	traditional	E
My Lord Will Come Again Joe Wise	*Gonna Sing, My Lord* (recording) WLP	R
Now Thank We All Our God Winkworth-Crueger	*People's Mass Book* WLP	R
Of My Hands Ray Repp	*Hymnal for Young Christians* FEL	O
Oh, How I Love Jesus Carey Landry	*Hi God* (recording) NALR	CS
Our Father Sister Janet Mead		S
Peace, Joy and Happiness Joe Wise	*Hand in Hand* (recording) WLP	R
Peace, My Friends Ray Repp	*Hymnal for Young Christians* FEL	R
Peace Time Carey Landry	*Hi God* (recording) NALR	E
Praise God Mary Braida	*God Made Us a Family* (recording) Mary Braida	S
Prayer for Peace Sebastian Temple	*Young People's Folk Hymnal* WLP	E
Prayer of St. Francis Lou Fortunate	*Songs for Confirmation* Wm. H. Sadlier	C
Prayer of St. Francis Sebastian Temple	*Young People's Folk Hymnal* WLP	OC
Put Your Hand in the Hand Gene MacLellan	Beechwood Music Corp. Hollywood, CA	ER
Raise Your Hands Jack Miffleton	*Come Out* (recording) WLP	RS

111

Rejoice in the Lord Always author unknown	*Hi God* (recording) NALR	S
The Seed Joe Wise	*Close Your Eyes, I Got a Surprise* (recording) NALR	E
Seek Ye First Mary Braida	*God Made Us a Family* (recording) Mary Braida	CS
She's Just an Old Stump Jack Miffleton	*Come Out* (recording) WLP	O
Shout From the Highest Mountain Ray Repp	*Hymnal for Young Christians* FEL	R
Sign of Peace Mary Braida	*God Made Us a Family* (recording) Mary Braida	CS
Simple Gifts Paul Page	*Songs for the Eucharist* Wm. H. Sadlier	O
Sing Joe Raposo	Warner Brothers Publications 1230 Avenue of the Americas New York, NY 10020	R
Sing Praise to the Lord Gregory Ballerino	*Worship Hymnal* GIA	E
Sons of God James Thiem	*Hymnal for Young Christians* FEL	C
Spirit of God Miriam Theresa Winter	*Joy Is Like the Rain* (recording) Vanguard	R
Stand Up! Jack Miffleton	*Even a Worm* (recording) WLP	S
Sunshine in My Soul Gregory Ballerino	*Worship Hymnal* GIA	E
Take Our Bread Joe Wise	*Young People's Folk Hymnal* WLP	O
Thank You Van Der Haas-Van Lelyveld	*Folk Hymnal for the Now Generation* Zondervan	O
Thank You Hymn Robert Blue	*Hymnal for Young Christians* FEL	R
Thanks for the Chance Joe Wise	*Close Your Eyes, I Got a Surprise* (recording) NALR	S
That's What Love Is Mary Braida	*God Made Us a Family* (recording) Mary Braida	CR

112

They'll Know We Are Christians P. Scholtes	*Hymnal for Young Christians* FEL	C
This Is the Day Cyril A. Reilly	*Hymnal for Young Christians* FEL	E
This Land Is Your Land Woody Guthrie	Ludlow Music Publishing 10 Columbia Circle New York, NY 10019	R
This Little Light anonymous	*Songs for Penance* Wm. H. Sadlier	C
To Be a Friend Jack Miffleton	*Come Out* (recording) WLP	S
The Visit Joe Wise	*Close Your Eyes, I Got a Surprise* (recording) NALR	S
We All Need One Another Lou Fortunate	*Songs for the Eucharist* Wm. H. Sadlier	E
Welcome in Joe Wise	*Welcome In* (recording) NALR	E
What Color Is God's Skin T. Wilkes and D. Stevenson	*Hi God* (recording) NALR	R
What Makes Love Grow Carey Landry	*Hi God* (recording) NALR	R
Whatsoever You Do W. F. Jabusch	*Hymnal for Young Christians* FEL	C
When the Saints Go Marching in traditional	traditional	E
Wonder-Full World James Thiem	*Hymnal for Young Christians* FEL	E
Yes to You Joe Wise	*Close Your Eyes, I Got a Surprise* (recording) NALR	OC
You Are My People Germaine Habjan	*Hymnal for Young Christians* FEL	S
You Fill the Day Joe Wise	*Young People's Folk Hymnal* WLP	OR

Music Publishers

Agape, Main Place, Carol Stream, IL 60187

Mary Braida, 1009 W. Marion, Knoxville, IA 50138

FEL — F.E.L. Publications, Ltd., 1925 Pontius Ave., Los Angeles, CA 90025

GIA — G.I.A. Publications, 2115 W. 63rd St., Chicago, IL 60636.

NALR — North American Liturgy Resources, 300 E. McMillan St., Cincinnati, OH 45219

William H. Sadlier, Inc., 11 Park Place, New York, NY 10007

Vanguard Music Corporation, 250 W. 57th St., New York, NY 10019

WLP — World Library Publications, 2145 Central Parkway, Cincinnati, OH 45214

Word, Inc., Box 1790, Waco, TX 76703

Zondervan Corporation, Grand Rapids, MI 49506

III. BIBLIOGRAPHY

Special mention should be made of two lectionaries suitable for children's liturgies, *A Children's Lectionary* and *Lectionary for Children's Mass*.

John Behnke, a Paulist deacon, has rewritten the readings of the Sunday lectionary cycles in language which children can understand. The Cycle A readings were published in 1974; the other two cycles will follow. *A Children's Lectionary* is published by Paulist Press, New York.

Aldo J. Tos starts with the New American Bible translation of the Sunday lectionary cycles, and edits the selections or chooses alternate texts when the standard readings are beyond the comprehension of children. *Lectionary for Children's Mass: Cycle A* was published in 1974 by Pueblo Publishing Company, New York.

Blandford, Elizabeth, S.C.N., Janet Marie Bucher, C.D.P., Neil Blunt and Jack Miffleton. *Come Out*. A liturgical kit consisting of a celebration book, song book and recording. Cincinnati, Ohio: World Library Publications, 1971.

Blandford, Elizabeth, S.C.N., and Jack Miffleton. *Even a Worm*. A liturgical kit consisting of a celebration book, a story book, song book and recording. Cincinnati, Ohio: World Library Publications, 1973.

Bradford, Barbara Taylor (ed.). *Children's Stories of the Bible from the Old and New Testaments*. New York: G R Book Company, Playmore, Inc., 1968.

Bremm, M.M. *The Man Caught by a Fish*. St. Louis: Arch Books, Concordia Publishing, 1967.

Bucher, Janet Marie, C.D.P. *Run With Him*. Cincinnati, Ohio: North American Liturgy Resources, 1974.

Deiss, Lucien and Gloria Weyman. *Dancing for God*. Cincinnati, Ohio: World Library Publications.

Directory for Masses with Children. Sacred Congregation for Divine Worship. Washington, D.C.: United States Catholic Conference, 1973.

Fahey, Benen, O.F.M. (trans.). *The Writings of St. Francis of Assisi.* With notes by Placid Hermann, O.F.M. Chicago: Franciscan Herald Press, 1964.

Faucher, W. Thomas and Ione C. Nieland. *Touching God.* Notre Dame, Ind.: Ave Maria Press, 1975.

Gallen, John (ed.). *Eucharistic Liturgies.* Paramus, N.J.: Paulist-Newman Press, 1969.

Hillmann, W., O.F.M. (ed.). *Children's Bible.* Translated by Lawrence Atkinson. Collegeville, Minn.: Liturgical Press, 1960

Hoey, Robert F. *The Experimental Liturgy Book.* New York: Seabury Press, 1969.

Jones, Charles E. *Way of the Cross Today for Children.* Notre Dame, Ind.: Ave Maria Press, 1968.

Kinghorn, Carol Jean and Carey Landry. *Hi God.* A liturgical kit consisting of a teacher-parent guide, posters, music book and recording. Cincinnati, Ohio: North American Liturgy Resources, 1973.

Le Blanc, Etienne and Mary Rose Talbot, C.I.C. *How Green Is Green?* Notre Dame, Ind.: Ave Maria Press, 1973.

Moser, Lawrence, E.S.J. *Home Celebrations.* Paramus, N.J.: Newman Press, 1970.

Parsons, William E., Jr. *Silly Putty and Other Children's Sermons.* Nashville: Abingdon, 1973.

Pottebaum, Gerald. *Story of Christmas.* Dayton, Ohio: Pflaum Publishing.

Rabalais, Sister Maria and Rev. Howard Hall. *Children, Celebrate!* Paramus, N.J.: Paulist Press, 1974.

Silverstein, Shil. *The Giving Tree.* New York: Harper and Row, 1964.

116

Sloyan, Virginia and Gabriel Huck. *Children's Liturgies.* Washington, D.C.: The Liturgical Conference.

Sloyan, Virginia. *Signs, Songs and Stories: Another Look at Children's Liturgies.* Washington, D.C.: The Liturgical Conference, 1974.

A Time for Living: Religious Experience Program. Nine volumes for each of four age categories. New York: Herder and Herder, 1972.

Weisheit, Eldon. *Sixty-one Gospel Talks for Children.* St. Louis: Concordia Publishing, 1969.

Weisheit, Eldon. *Sixty-one Worship Talks for Children.* St. Louis: Concordia Publishing.

IV. CHECKLIST FOR PREPARING THE LITURGY

Prepared by _____

Mass theme _____

_____

Explanation before Mass given by _____

Entrance procession _____

Banner _____

Made by _____ Carried by _____

Opening hymn _____

Penitential rite _____

Reading I _____ Read by _____

Responsorial _____ Led by _____

Reading II _____ Read by _____

Alleluia _____ Led by _____

Reading III _____

Homily _____

Prayers of the faithful prepared by_____

Read by_____

Offertory procession _____

Offertory hymn _____

Eucharistic prayer _____

Eucharistic acclamation (sung or recited) _____

Great amen (sung or recited) _____

Our Father (sung or recited) _____

Sign of peace _____

Communion hymn: _____

Recessional _____